8 META
(BECAUSE THE 1
IS NOT A ⌐⌐ʋʌ)

TABLE OF CONTENTS

FOREWORD

Established in 2007 and funded by the Leverhulme Trust, the LUX Associate Artists Programme is a one-year, post-academic professional development programme for artists who make moving image works, where the moving image is considered an integral and vital component of the visual arts. Eight practicing artists are selected from around 120 applications to take part in a series of twelve monthly group meetings, each attended by an invited guest speaker, personal mentorships, extracurricular discussions and activities.

Configured as a group of artists with different practices, interests, voices and experience, the year-round discussion is driven by a combination of participants (and guests) who present ideas that have a particular, personal currency in an attempt to articulate individual positions, while also sharing or interrogating these things with/by others in a conscious act of questioning and self-reflection. As a framework, the AAP is an ambitious 'learning' model: it is as much a situation as it is a proposed structure, the terms of which are continuously negotiated and contested. Such negotiations are in and of themselves an extension – if not a materialisation – of the enquiry into what we do, why, how we speak it, understand it and how we might use a more generous multiplicity of perspectives for the sake of ongoing production.

In addition, each year the challenge for participants is to find ways of reflecting (and reflecting upon) their experience of the programme in a final public project of their own devising. This book, produced by the participants of 2008/9, is the result of a serious and exhaustive exploration of just what kind of form such a challenge might take. It is a collection of eight positions made visible by and read through a multiplicity of others, a group work of many documents, a testament to shared and separate experiences – a situation of productive refraction.

Our gratitude is due to all those who have made this possible, with thanks to the 2008/9 guest speakers: Robert Beavers, Stuart Comer, Chrissie Iles, Mary Kelly, Simon Martin, Rachel Moore, Maureen Paley, Mike Sperlinger, Catherine Sullivan, David Toop; and to the artists' mentors: John Akomfrah,

Steve Claydon, Ann Course, Adam Curtis, Cerith Wyn Evans, Andrea Geyer, Will Holder, Mark Leckey, Jeremy Millar, Gail Pickering, Elizabeth Price, Josephine Pryde, Lis Rhodes, Lucy Skaer, Stephen Sutcliffe; to all of the participating artists and contributors for their dedication; and especially to Isla Leaver-Yap whose indefatigable enthusiasm, intellectual sensitivity, engagement and energy exceed the page.

Ian White   Ben Cook
Facilitator, LUX   Associate Artists Programme Director, LUX

INTRODUCTION
Isla Leaver-Yap

During the first meeting for this book project, the eight artists of the Associate Artists Programme and I stumbled over an inherent and inescapable contradiction: what did this group, who work primarily with the moving image over any other medium, hope to achieve by making a book? After all, a book is a static form that largely dispenses with the cinematic issue of unitary time, the instantaneousness of video, and whose primary apparatus deals not in sound, colour, or image, but with text read at the timing and selection of its reader. More so, what did we expect to uncover by writing and editing this publication? How does an artists *write* their practice? These questions were not just the starting point for this project, but the principles upon which this book has been constructed.

Such questions are difficult to address in isolation, and it was clear from the beginning *8 Metaphors* should not only be an exercise in writing, but also an opportunity to commission external contributors with whom the artists might grapple with the idea of writing a practice. Thus the form of this book primarily comprises textual conversations between each artist and their chosen interlocutors, a host of individuals who bring their own expertise. It is significant, then, that these many contributors are from diverse disciplines: philosophers, psychotherapists, musicians, curators, shopkeepers, artists and scientists, to name but a few. These people form a loose network of collaborators for each artist and, importantly, they also occupy the role of an intimate and responsive audience.

Following this route of collaboration, embedded in each of the artists' chapters is an emphasis on the contingency of making and of making meaning: the need for verification, translation, reinscription by others. There is a tacit acknowledgement within these dialogues that a network of similar or sympathetic practices might share the responsibility and load of meaning, or might offer insights through their own interpretations. Laure Prouvost's engagement with a specifically non-art audience finds unexpected and expansive responses to her video *It, Heat, Hit,* for example, while Laura Gannon's work with psychotherapist Mina Bancheva offers a more personal insight into an otherwise sidelined aspect of the artist's practice.

Artistic meaning — perhaps better understood in terms of intentionality — is often cultivated within a milieu that is either artificially constructed (and this group of eight selected artists may be described as such) or socially assembled (as one might view Luke Fowler's work with Éric La Casa, Lee Patterson and Toshiya Tsunoda). But in both cases, the book highlights the attempt to identify meaning as a critical endeavour, where writing is used as a form of accountability and a cipher through which ideas surrounding practice and work might be transmitted to an outside audience/reader. This accountability or, perhaps more precisely, this visibility is what Emma Wolukau–Wanambwa describes in her chapter as the desire to "show one's working", a tenet central to this publication. From using the basic interview format to invite critical responses to one's practice (used in Stina Wirfelt's conversation with Deborah Stratman, and Samuel Stevens' letter exchange with Uriel Orlow), to exploring dialogue as a means to exchange ideas, inspirations and influence (evident in the *quid pro quo* of Duncan Marquiss and Lars Bang Larsen's 'Volley', or the play scripts of Grace Schwindt and Marina Vishmidt), such a format allows materials and ideas to be set in an analogic relationship with one another, to develop unlikely comparisons, frictions, or else find the richness in minor difference.

This correspondence between things is central: between artist and interlocutor (Gannon and Marquiss), practice and work (Fowler), thinking and making (Wolukau–Wanambwa), research and display (Schwindt and Wirfelt), artist and audience (Prouvost) and display and text (Stevens). But within these correspondences is also a healthy suspicion of the text as something that might adequately communicate. Stevens' texts ruminate on the loss and unlikely accrual of meaning in the process of translation. In his chapter, artist Maija Timonen remarks, "the image also seems to serve the purpose of writing the author out, of muffling the authorial voice", a tactic purposefully reversed by Stevens' ekphrastic 'stills' and dialogues, both written with his second interlocutor, Uriel Orlow. Wolukau–Wanambwa, meanwhile, presents a text full of glitches, stops, redactions, and insertions − a permeable text that is presented in progress, in a state of preponderance. The form of the printed word is presented in Schwindt's section as flux. In her scripts, routes of transcription, documentation, and reinterpretation move in a zigzag direction, proliferating meaning, and thus evading the political pressures of rhetoric and original context. Compiled, performed, transcribed by a stenographer, and re-edited, these compromised words find themselves scattered among implied architectures and physical environments.

It is perhaps not by coincidence that Wolukau−Wanambwa and Schwindt both use the script format as a means of expressing ideas that relate to their artistic process. The format is of course a 'play' of participants, actions, gestures and narrative drive. These scripts also allows for intriguing ambiguity: are these simply transcriptions of a dialogue, or is there something about the form that implies a repeatability, a setting up or prescription of action? The script form, although potentially part of a film practice, is here suggested as the revelation of methodology, occupying the contrasting roles of development and delivery. It is, as Wolukau−Wanambwa points out at one point, "thinking, research, development … everything happened at the same time".

Taking these notions of simultaneous thinking and making in a different direction altogether are the presentations of Marquiss and Fowler. Marquiss' close relationship to and investigations of Romanticism has long been a key to his practice. His desire to cultivate a primarily visual language to articulate the liminal space between the experience of reality and the representation of myth is transformed to text in his contribution to this book. It is significant that Lars Bang Larsen's invitation to participate as both collaborator with and player to Marquiss is not a casual choice; Larsen's curatorial and writing practices often probe the transgressive potential of the hallucinatory and the gothic imagination, and the ways in which the limits of experience might serve as the space of artistic inscription. Together, Marquis and Larsen present a to-and-fro of quotations, which serve as nodes of expansion and diversion, while also seeking to chart a common vernacular for their fugitive yet concentrated contact.

Fowler's approach to this book, on the other hand, already echoes the workings of his previous body of films and collaborators. Thinking through A *Grammar For Listening*, a collaboration with three sound artists that seeks to synthesise sound and image, Fowler's chapter transposes the prior image and sound collaboration into a series of text reflections, a collaborative matrix score, and a dialogue with the writer and theorist Christoph Cox. The texts map key points of the collaborative endeavours – including questions of the political and social reality of the act of recording, as well as the possibility of such works casting light on what Fowler identifies as "the fraught ecology of our present condition".

While the integrity of the recording process is challenged by some, Prouvost intentionally seeks out what she describes as "the complex and extended (mis)understanding" of her work. Inviting responses from a host of non-art professionals by showing them her video *It, Heat, Hit*, Prouvost's chapter surveys a diversity of opinion, revealing the intriguing tendency for her contributors' to interpret her work through the lens of their own profession. Her chapter demonstrates the limitations of an art-savvy audience and its vernacular, and the responses open up a series of new directions for work.

Gannon's project, by contrast, commits to a single non-art professional for guidance. Using a psychotherapist to arrive at the interpretations of specific works, Gannon's chapter ruminates on childhood memory, the notion of home, and the artist's use of recurring motif in relation to her drawing – an aspect of her practice she seeks to consider more holistically in relation to her filmmaking. With echoes of Freud's paper 'Remembering, Repeating and Working Through', Gannon examines the unconscious motives at work in her practice, and presents her investigations as a generous and inquisitive act.

Where Gannon's project is an inward reflection, Wirfelt's project is cast out into the world, and probes the notion of virtual space and the anonymous dandy as rendered (most recently) in Google Streetview. Inviting her interlocutors to consider this as a temporally uncertain terrain, not to mention a politically charged environment, Wirfelt reveals her perspective on the spatial breaches that an artist might seek out and claim as the space of practice. Interestingly,

Wirfelt's chapter begins with a deferral of authorship: an anonymous text entitled 'The Joker', that posits agency as a characteristic of the artist, and contemplates the moves available to a maverick.

There are few images among these pages, and almost no images of the artists' previous work. Despite (or perhaps because of) the popular tradition of printing still images of moving image work in art catalogues, monographs and survey publications both in print and online, it seemed necessary that *8 Metaphors* address the fact that still images are rarely the most advantageous format through which to convey the content of film and video. In a monograph, for instance, stills are typically relegated to the role of illustration, the content of which is always inadequately represented because the static form suppresses the singular aspect that differentiates film and video from other forms of art: motion. Stills tend to sell their subject (not to mention the artist's practice) short, falsely emphasising an event-fulness of one scene over all others, and are selected based on how 'good' or iconic the image might appear in printed form rather than for their truth to their original material. *8 Metaphors'* refusal to resort to the image as 'shorthand' is one of the defining qualities of this publication. Together, these chapters consciously reinscribe the space usually reserved for the specular or the illustrative image with textual content, or else use images as a textual device to map and score meaning.

At a point where the moving image is informally passed around via DVD showreels and internet transfer, transmitted through folders of jpegs and accessed through online streams, the need to find precise ways of describing and dealing with the content of the moving image *without being casual* is ever more pressing. *8 Metaphors* doesn't deny these conduits of information, nor linger on the nostalgia of medium specificity. Rather, it seeks to find a new space for dis-cussion where such debate, rendered in text, is critical to the complexity of work and the depth of an artist's practice.

A book with ambitions such as these would never have been possible without the faith, intelligence and passion of the artists, and the expertise and interest of the book's many contributors. Together, their words set out the dynamic and complex arguments of the book with uncompromising clarity, and emphasise the necessity for a publication such as this. For the artists' and contributors' trust and moving collaborations I am most grateful. Integral to any presentation, too, is the configuration of materials. The thoughtful book design has been delivered by HIT, who sympathetically configured a dense and heterogeneous series of texts with their characteristically deft style and energy. Warm thanks are also owed to Ian White and LUX whose unwavering support and shrewd advice began a long time prior to this publication, when these eight artists were first selected for the Associate Artists Programme in 2008. Ian and LUX's exceptional work and commitment — past, present, and future — is immeasurable.

LUKE FOWLER WITH
ÉRIC LA CASA, LEE PATTERSON
AND TOSHIYA TSUNODA

REFLECTIONS ON
A GRAMMAR

TRANSITIONAL WORDS
Luke Fowler

In his article on the 'acousmatic', Pierre Schaeffer introduces a major philosophical premise of *musique concrète*. The concept of the acousmatic, a term Schaeffer gleans from the Larousse dictionary, is invoked through an aphorism: the story of Pythagoras lecturing to his disciples over a five year period, hidden from view, with his voice projecting from behind a curtain. Thus, the acousmatic is a sound event or phenomena stripped of external (and visual) reference. The apparent zeal with which Schaeffer appropriated this term for his own rhetoric cannot be fully understood without first appreciating the conditions that gave rise to the birth of this radical new music. Indeed *musique concrète* was perhaps the first musical form that fully disposed with the cult of celebrity. It eschewed the holy trinity of conductor, performer and musical instrument, and replaced these roles with the tools of the microphone and tape recorder, and the resultant sound disseminated either through the then-emerging technology of radio, or via concerts featuring multiple loudspeaker diffusions.

I'm prepared to assert, speaking from a Scottish perspective, that the radicality of this act has yet to be fully rehearsed. What I and many other artists are attracted to in *musique concrète* is Schaeffer's idea of 'reduced listening', a term that encourages the listener to focus on the phenomenal characteristics of sound (as opposed to its musical or cultural significations), a focus that results in a richer experience of music and its constituent parts (sonorous objects). Schaeffer also emphasises the need to describe and analyse the collective 'subjectivity' of sound objects, which leads one to a deeper, universal understanding of the nature of sound.

It is not without due caution, then, that I set about making a cycle of films which took the complex act of field recording as a starting point. Upon establishing my collaborators for these films — Lee Patterson, Éric La Casa and Toshiya Tsunoda (an incomplete *Part 4* was also shot with Sean Meehan) — I put forward a number central questions: to what degree could Schaeffer's 'reduced listening' (a concept that seems to be one of the central tenets of field recording) be achieved when 'accompanied' by the moving image; would the moving image become superfluous, a mere visual banality, or could it give sound more depth; could there then be a 'reduced viewing', a viewing which renounces the usual secondary status of sound in film, in order to establish equal footing with that of the image; is there an underlying political and social reality repressed by the field recorder in the act of gathering their exotic sound souvenirs; can the union between sound and image cast a light on the fraught ecology of our present condition? Such enquiries hint at the complex realities underneath the surface of Schaeffer's 'pure listening'.

In 'The Despotism of The Eye', Irish Poet and critic Tom Paulin recounts an early childhood memory of listening to a haunting whistling sound while lying awake in bed and being mesmerised by the beauty of the 'acousmatic' experience. As an adult, he later discovers the origin of this sound phenomenon to be the wind blowing through the metal fence posts in Ormeau Park, Ireland. He comments that sounds can have all sorts of ontological meanings, adding, "it is to do with our dwelling in the world, our being. It is to do with, as it were, our ontology of relationship, which we have with the entire universe".

CROSS-COLLABORATIONS
Lee Patterson

If memory serves me correctly, *A Grammar For Listening* began life as a slightly different entity. After working together on his film *Bogman Palmjaguar* during the summer of 2007, Luke suggested a new project based around my work and approach to field recording. With this in mind, later that same summer I asked Luke if he could assist me during a separate project in Argyll.

Barry Esson of Arika had selected both Toshiya Tsunoda and myself to create environmentally sited works for an outdoor event. During the research and installation phases we needed a driver to take us to various locations. I suggested to Luke that if he could drive it could be an ideal opportunity for him to gather material and to meet Toshiya.

Throughout 2008, we collaborated on other projects, including the series of films/performances *Draw a straight line and follow it*. Luke also initiated his ongoing collaboration with Toshiya. Additionally, there were discussions about *Ontology of Sound*, as the project was then called. Luke had formulated certain ideas as to what the project should set out to achieve and how it might then progress. It became clear that it would not focus on my work alone, which admittedly was something of a relief.

Given our mutual understanding of each other's approaches (and sometimes lack thereof — there were occasional disagreements over the course of the project), it was decided that we should attempt to transcribe or cross-apply the ideas behind our respective working techniques. Luke began using his camera in a similar fashion to how I might use certain microphones and vice versa; we worked within environments or locations and with objects or processes that suited this type of cross-collaboration. Luke was particularly interested in the visual properties of the burning nuts I often use in live performance and I showed him the wave forms traced by a point light source within vibrating springs — a phenomenon I had wanted to document for some years.

During 2009, we visited locations along the Clyde and others near Callander as well as the motorway junction and a hill top location near my home in order to gather material. Due to the limitations and varying conditions that affect recording outcomes, I insisted upon locations with particular features, such as water bodies and resonant structures. My perception at the time (due to many places being saturated with vehicular noise) was that it would be easier to find interesting visual material than sonic, much to Luke's occasional annoyance I'm sure.

Either way, in spite of the challenges or perhaps because of them, I like to think of *A Grammar For Listening* as our must successful collaboration to date. We attempted to work against the flow of conventional acousmatic and cinematic practice, and formulated new approaches to listening and looking via the acts of recording and filming.

THE TEMPLE RECORDING
Toshiya Tsunoda

I make recordings by going to a location and finding an intriguing object. I take a stethoscope containing a miniature built-in air microphone, and place the ear tips of the stethoscope on the temples of my head. The stethoscope captures the vibrations of my muscles and the blood flow in my head. Environmental noises are also captured by the microphone; if the wind blows it will be recorded as it passes over my head.

The recording often resembles the sound you hear if you block your ears with your fingers.

The microphone can be positioned anywhere near the ears, but I think the temples are the best place for making a sound recording. There is no relation between the temples, an air microphone and brain waves; our brain waves do not stir the air.

In some ways, this method could be described as a field recording. Abstract issues other than field recordings are also involved here, of course, such as my intentionality and its object. But at the very least, one can call this recording 'evidence' of my focusing in on an object at a certain place and time.

I recently used a second stethoscope on another person's temples. The two of us sat side by side, recording, focusing on the landscape. Together, we created a stereo 'sound image'. A landscape becomes a more distinct object with the perceptions of two people rather than one — a 'fuller' recording can emerge from such a scenario. The main issue here is our grasp of the image: capturing a single image with two inputs — something that our eyes and ears normally perform.

With the 'space information' — sent from two persons' ears to our brains — neither of us can distinguish our individually perceived sounds. This stereo sound image is created between and through both people. If two people face the same landscape each may have different experiences. But in this activity, there is no doubt that those two people shared the same landscape. Their experiences are set inside the recording.

THE MAP AND THE GROUND
Éric La Casa

When exploring territories as vast and dense as Paris or Glasgow, a topographic map allows for all layers and their realities to be smoothed out into a single drawing, as precise in its measurements as it is schematic. This is why two-dimensional representation is often the first tool used to make contact with a terrain. With a single glance, we seize the geography of a country and extrapolate its possibilities.

The sketch is a trigger to our mental construction of the spaces through which we begin to make our way, and onto which we bring our attention to bear. This reflexive examination of the map — be it a strict adherence to scientific data, or else a surrendering of oneself to non-geographic interpretations — directs the mind towards a series of hypotheses that simulate one's arrival on the ground, sometimes determining the very nature of the in-situ project (when, for example, one encounters terrains that have remarkable features).

The map's ordered vision releases one from the complexities of reality and establishes a clear scope for observation; it provides a vantage point from which interdisciplinary dialogue is possible. Thus, an abandoned military area, a valley downstream of a dam, a business district built on a concrete slab or an old towpath become spaces where one sees the promise of a unique encounter or, more simply put, of interesting encounters, whether sonic, visual, or other.

Once there, the map's promises are surveyed not by methodology but by the body, as one drifts along unpremeditated trajectories. Without method or compass one wanders like an animal, senses awakened, before arriving at an exact position where microphones and / or cameras can validate and record a particular space / time. This 'particularity' is linked to strategies of movement (one's relation to the landscape's constants, for instance), climatic fluctuations (and their attendant consequences) and everything that resists understanding; our alerted senses attempt to grasp such things.

The result is an accumulation of recordings; an environment is put to the test, networks and relationships operate according to various rules. It is a location-based composition that takes into account measurements from one site only, rather than simultaneous mixes of elements from different sites. Together, the recordings form a representation of the world, a precise environment whose aesthetic expression nestles close to cartography.

A MATRIX SCORE

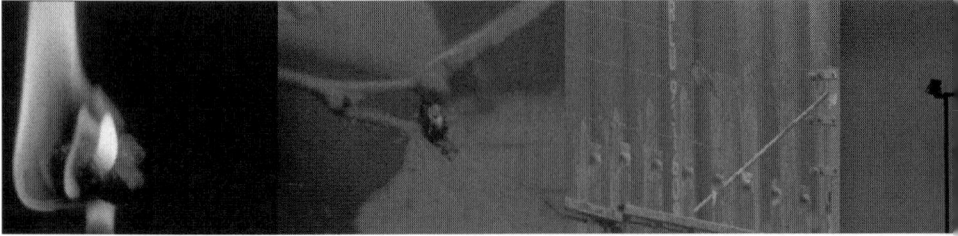

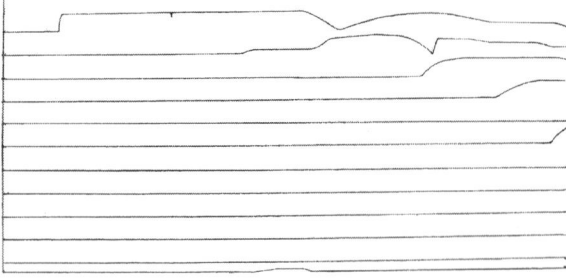

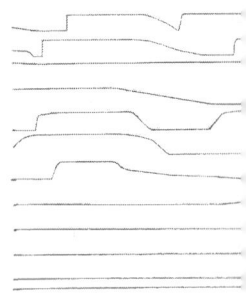

II. VIBRATIONS IN AIR,
WATER AND SOLIDS
WITH SURFACE REFLECTIONS

VI. SOUND WAVES
AS LIGHTFORMS

III. PASSING REFLECTIONS
& REFRACTIONS IN AIR
& WATER

6:30 7:00 9:30 10:00 10:30 11:00   16:30 17:00 17:30 18:00 18:30 19:00 19:30 20:00 20:30 21:00 21:30 22:00

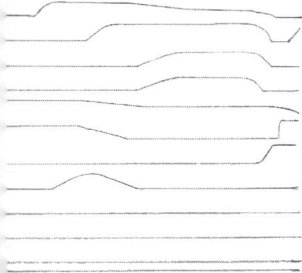

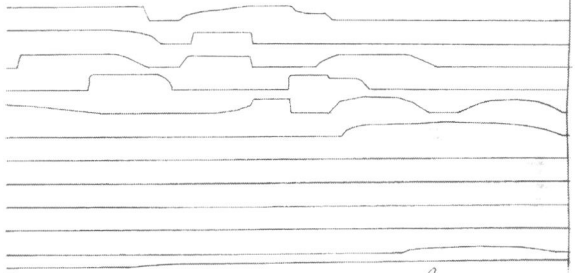

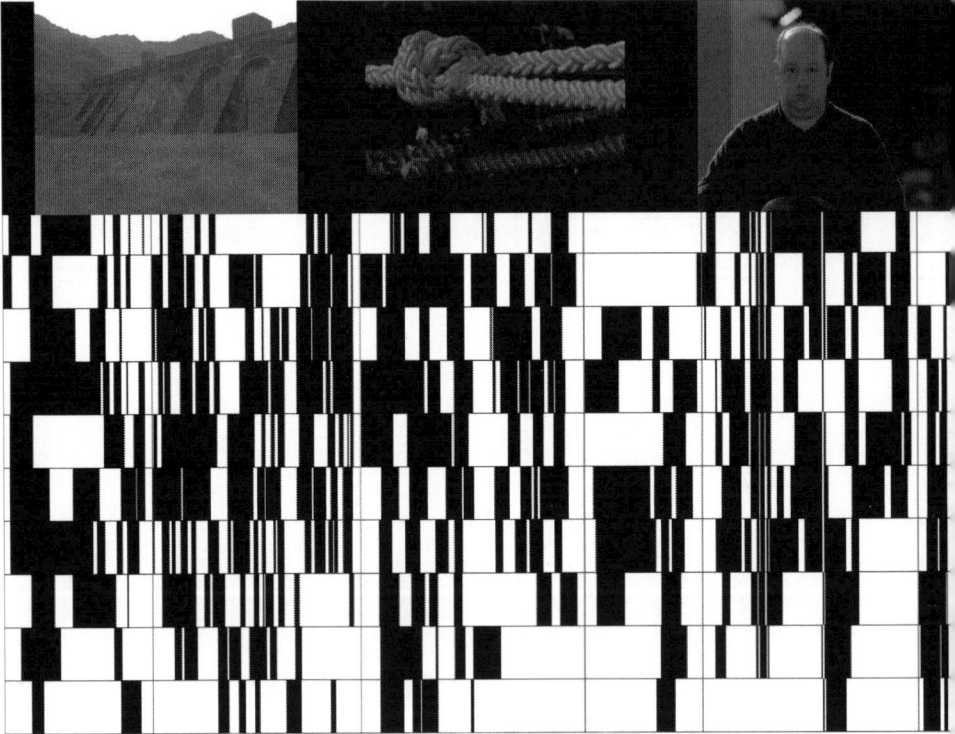

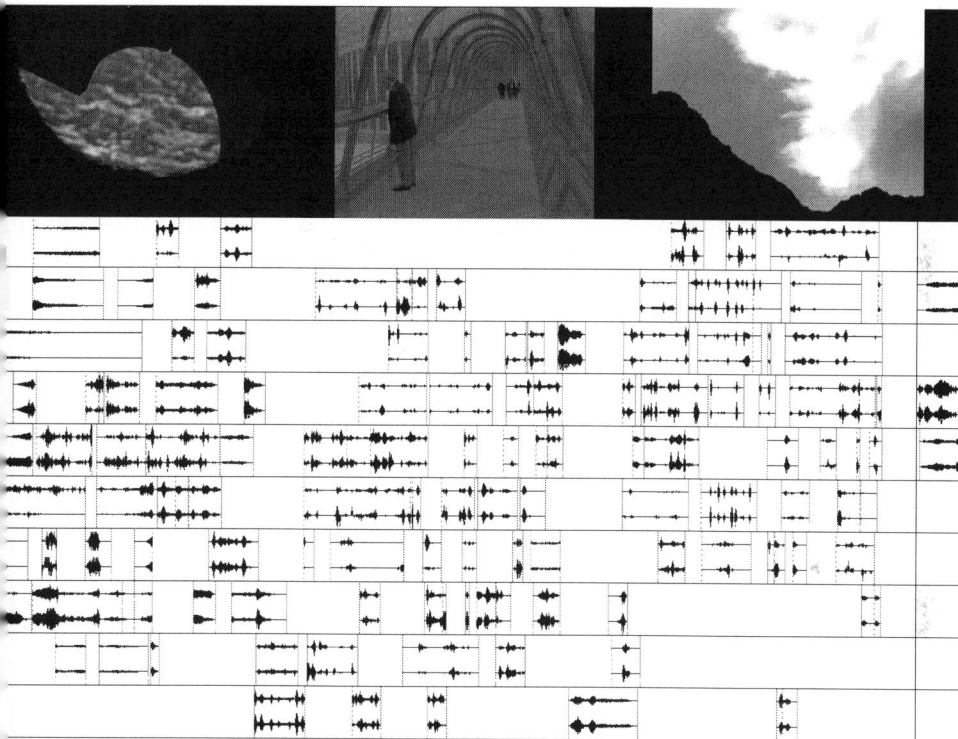

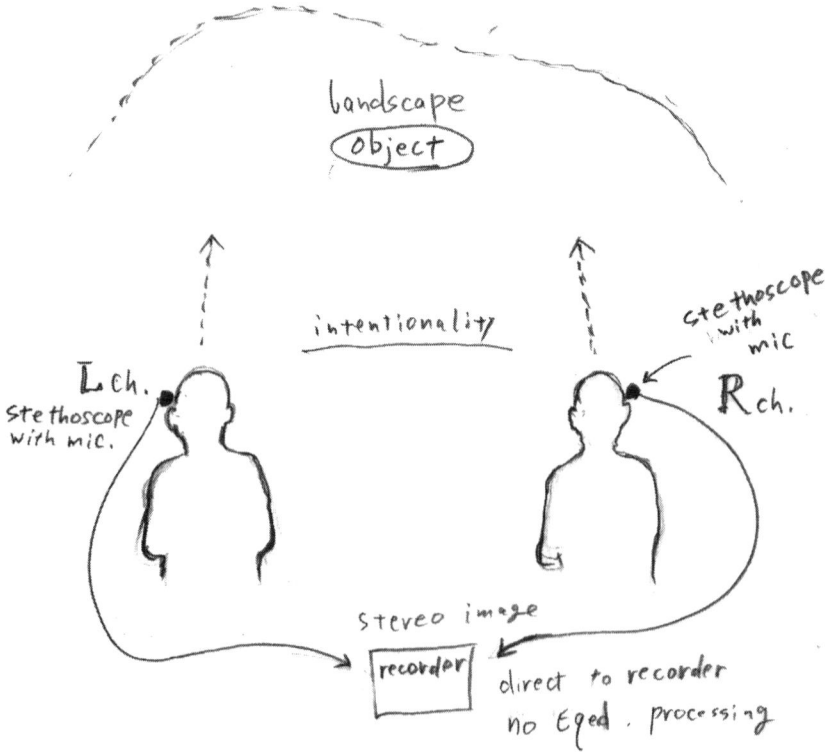

landscape
(object)

intentionality

L ch.
ste thoscope
with mic.

stethoscope
with
mic

R ch.

stereo image
recorder

direct to recorder
no Eqed . processing

INTERVIEWS with CHRISTOPH COX

ÉRIC LA CASA

CHRISTOPH COX: To what degree are you trying to document particular sounds in relation or in contrast to trying to produce an art object? Are these tendencies distinct in your work?

ÉRIC LA CASA: A project is always given a specific response. From the original idea, the process to be employed is tested and, as a result, it is validated (or not) in situ. Using methods derived from the humanities, the concept is tested in the field in order to bring about questions that couldn't and shouldn't be predetermined. That is why I increasingly find myself employing work protocols (a more scientific method) in order to examine the project with the hope this methodology will allow all possible 'lessons' to be drawn. The working protocol can be deduced from the terrain but may sometimes be linked to a driving principle only. For example, the fact that Luke uses a 16 mm camera with only a short length of film stock — about 3 minutes and 30 seconds, if I remember correctly — instructs the whole process. Each parameter is a calculation that determines the future form of the work.

Your question implies another, which concerns my relationship with the question of artistic taste. This is key in the discussion of methodology. How do my personal tastes — including all possible internal conflicts — impact on my work during all the stages of the process? To what extent is my work protocol protected from my preconceived approach to the terrain, to the way I hear it?

CC: When you record, what do you listening for? What sounds attract you?

ÉLC: I don't have a system (of listening) that can be employed for all sites. My ways of listening are adapted to each project and to the different questions posed. If I'm taken particularly by the (acoustic) qualities of a space. I don't impose preconceived ideas on what I ought to encounter in that space. The map serves as a medium for hypotheses and opens up perspectives that, once surveyed, will define a form. In any case, I always try to put myself in the service of the project.

With Luke, our principal idea was to work on everyday environments. We weren't looking for the extraordinary — this is a feature in our respective work. The key was to be able to go in one direction and be free to interact according to our own rules (technical, temporal etc.). Each of us led or influenced the other in terms of possible sites and reactions. In Paris, I chose exclusively car-free spaces in order to preserve the location's acoustic properties (among others): the Seine under Pont Alexandre III, around the Grande Arche at La Défense, the Parc Floral and its greenhouses, a bike path along the Ourcq Canal. All of these places allowed us to deploy our different devices and to individually record that which seems specific to that site. To speak only of sound: the grinding of barge ropes and the distant murmur of the city, the alternation of near-nothings and crashing trains, under the various railway bridges, footsteps reverberating in the underground corridors of the Grande Arche — none of this was pre-meditated. The aesthetic project alone gave birth to the desire to record these specific locations. I made choices based on the map and on my own knowledge of the area, sites whose heterophony might wrong-foot our preconceptions and our inventions, thematic inventions included. Based on this overflow of sounds, we had to invent another way of reading the landscape and of deducing a form.

CC: What, for you, is the specificity of audio or sound? Can sound capture something that, for example, film can't?

ÉLC: It always seems to me a little misleading to speak of the specificity of a medium if one works only in that medium. I can't make comparisons, given that I only use sound. It's a question of attention or of listening, if you prefer. I don't think I'm more sensitive or receptive to sound; but because I work mainly with my ears I can say this sense is perhaps a little more developed, a little more educated. When a film works well, we don't ask whether the visuals take precedence over sound, we enter the film's world without making the distinction. Whatever medium I use to survey a landscape, I develop an attention measured by my instrument's capabilities and by what is opened up to me by my consciousness. I mention perception because my work resides first and foremost in this sensory approach. Be it a camera, a microphone, my fingers or my nose, I choose a tool that allows me access to a phenomenological territory. Decisions made within the framework of a work protocol, and the levels of perception / consciousness, are the project's true motors. In other words, I invent paths that lead to destinations unknown at the time of their invention.

LEE PATTERSON

CHRISTOPH COX: You've described your work as "eavesdropping upon events that are both alien yet utterly quotidian". This nicely captures two different tendencies in your work. On the one hand, you proceed in an almost documentary fashion, meticulously recording the sounds of objects around you and presenting them virtually untreated. On the other hand, you use these sounds as a way to transport the listener out of the mundane world, to make it strange or to open up alien, exotic dimensions. Are these two tendencies naturally conjoined for you, or is there some tension between them?

LEE PATTERSON: They're usually different aspects of the same activity and owe their existence to this common origin. However, tension may arise in the way they naturally push and pull against each other. Sounds and objects which have unexpected qualities and complexities are of most interest to me, where the dynamic between the expected and the exotic or, more correctly, the unfamiliar is greatest. With experience, I've come to expect the presence of certain sounds within particular things, so this has led to a normalisation whereby the alien and the familiar co-exist in different ways.

My aim isn't so much to transport a listener out of the mundane world but allow them to go further into it, to demonstrate just how strange and unfamiliar it can be upon closer inspection, and to make it less mundane and more engaging, thus mirroring or sharing some of my own experiences. This may be read as an aesthetic quest into realms previously inaccessible (for me) or it could be nothing more than a call to pay more attention, to develop a greater sensitivity in order to force a change in the current order of things. How the latter may be effectively achieved, and indeed whether or not it should be, is still a challenge.

CC: To what degree is this conjunction of the quotidian and the exotic dependent on the technological set-up? I mean, microphones can attune us to sounds going on around us but they also allow us to hear what the 'naked ear' cannot, making a microscopic access to the world possible.

LP: Borrowing from Marshall McLuhan, amplification and recording technology is not only a fixative agent but it can also be considered an extension of the nervous system. But despite this enhancement (or perhaps because of it), different strategies have to be used when listening to the amplified world, as the ears differentiate in ways the microphone does not. After experiencing the enhancements offered by microphones and recording devices, what happens to the naked ear and its associated psychoacoustic devices? From personal experience, I'd say that one is left with an enhanced appreciation or ability to hear, to listen as if one were recording. There is a feedback between the aided and the naked ear, whereby ears are trained through the act of recording and listening can become a post-technological act.
Though it's a useful term and many of my listening / recording activities concern themselves with small or virtually inaudible sounds, I'm a little wary of thinking about them as microscopic or 'audio as microscopy'. It's too much of a visually-biased term. Likewise, I'm dubious about the use of the term 'field recording', the origins of which lie within a more directly musical tradition. Maybe it should be referred to as environmental audiography or auscultation (to borrow from the medical lexicon).

CC: How do you determine which sounds and recordings are valuable, worth pursuing and releasing as recordings?

LP: Whether or not a sound blows me away, whether a recording is more than the sum of its parts, these relate to my earlier comments regarding the dynamic ratio between familiar and unexpected sound material. Has something seemingly unusual been heard? Does it sound 'exotic' or unfamiliar, both within the sonic environment in which it's heard and in reference to personal experience? Does the sound reveal information or provide evidence of an otherwise concealed action or phenomenon?

I once made a contact microphone recording of a candle. It was quiet and, tonally, it was also texturally uninteresting. Yet it revealed something I couldn't otherwise have known: at regular intervals the activity increased, suggesting the flame burnt the moulton wax in a cyclic pattern that was invisible but could be heard when more liquid wax was drawn up into the wick, contrary to what I expected from listening to other things burn.

What are the aesthetic qualities of the sound? What are the recording's timbral, textural and tonal qualities and complexities? Does it have musical qualities? Obviously, my ears have been informed by certain musical forms as well as by the act of listening via microphones, recorders and amplifiers. Sounds I find interesting may reflect this in a number of ways, by their similarity to or distinction from things I've heard before.

In terms of pursuing a sound-making mechanism, how much variation exists? How different is the sound of a particular process each time it's conducted or encountered? Is the variation sufficiently different to attempt multiple recordings? I might wish to document an interesting acoustic space or acoustic properties thereof as activated by resident sound. There might be physical actions present at a location that generate sound upon the introduction of a contact microphone or hydrophone and these may yield interesting material according to some of the considerations mentioned here.

There are also questions regarding whether a sound has been heard before or whether, as far as I'm aware, a sound-making activity has been done or recorded by someone else. On a more technical level, the quality of a recording is important. The signal to noise ratio, whether unwanted sounds are audible in the recording — if a recording is intended to explore this relationship, is there a clear distinction between that indicates this?

How one determines value and interest in a sound or recording is a tough question to answer. Perhaps the considerations above are just a few of the things one has to bear in mind when out and about listening and recording.

LUKE FOWLER

CHRISTOPH COX: I'm interested in the relationships between image and sound in *A Grammar for Listening.* The image track gives the soundtrack a concreteness, a focus for the sounds, the sources of which are often hard to place. But your image rarely delivers or matches the sonic sources.

LUKE FOWLER: The impetus behind *A Grammar* was to create a series of works that existed outside of verbal language. One of my intentions was to bring sound and certain 'sound artists' to the fore, a desire that surfaced because of my own involvement with and excitement about currents in field recording and experimental music. The concrete experience of working with Lee Patterson on *Bogman Palmjaguar* (in which his role as composer / sound recordist is equally important as the main protagonists) was a great influence.

I set about making some initial 16mm and video studies, which captured Lee and Toshiya Tsunoda 'documentary' style on recording trips, discussing their work and so on. But I quickly realised that this initial concept was weak and needed reconsideration. I wanted to find a new form for these ideas, to completely erase text as a way into the films, and thus work counter to my previous work that relied heavily upon the voice to provide a narrative (often through interviews and archival material).

This decision — that the image could stand alone — was greatly indebted to discovering the films of Robert Beavers and having the privilege to discuss them, and my own past work, with him. In Beavers' work the spirit of a place, or a series of metaphors and associations, are carefully crafted across a highly rhythmic and formally innovative image and soundtrack. They are really remarkable works that deserve to be far more widely discussed and appreciated.

I was interested in taking this premise of re-instating the image. But, in doing so, I did not want to relegate the role of sound to a second-order function. In 2008, I attended a field recording workshop with sound recordist Chris Watson. It was clear from his work that one needed to respect the difference between working with sound and with image. For a start, they require two very different types of attention and different times of the day to capture a phenomenon. It became increasingly apparent that to fully respect the role of sound in film, it was necessary for me to create a series of dialogues with artists who devote their lives to sound as an art form.

CC: In what ways did working with sound artists affect your decisions about what to film and how to edit your footage?

LF: This is two-fold. Firstly, as these works were collaborative, all the main decisions — from the concept to location and final edit — were generally agreed upon together. In each pairing, we took turns to host the other in our home city, taking the other to places that each felt would be rewarding for the other. I recall Lee getting very excited about the hydrophone recordings he made in Greenock, while Éric La Casa seemed to get some fantastic results from the winds that picked up and excited the steel barriers at the top of Loch Sloy. I would rarely, as you point out, want to film the sound's source — like, say, those steel barriers — partly because we didn't want to have hard syncs, but also because it seemed quite futile. Sound recording and filming often work with phenomena that are quite distinct: the camera is limited to documenting light across surfaces, while a microphone can record something miles away, transduce vibrations deep within a surface, or record sounds often imperceptible to the senses.
So, although we collaborated, we also trusted one another to find something of equivalent importance, which was difficult at times. But it was also in those times I found I was really struggling to 'see' something, that my interaction with the camera, the place, and the situation would coalesce. The rushes from those moments would completely surpass my expectations.

TOSHIYA TSUNODA

CHRISTOPH COX: Until recently, your work as an audio artist attempted to capture the vibrations of various objects and to map the vibrational contexts of particular spaces. Your new work seems to shift the focus towards the body of the listener — or towards your body as an artist. What led you to this shift of focus and what do you hope to gain by this new approach?

TOSHIYA TSUNODA: My new way of working, which I call 'Temple Recording', is not focused on the body and listening. Rather, I'm interested in the relationship between intentionality and its object. I often record the condition of a space and then try to find another way to describe it. A body — a person with stethoscope on his or her temples — is like an arrow pointing at something.

For me, the 'field' in field recording does not simply mean physical place. Place or space always depends on one's consideration. We can think of a house as a particular place; a public park is a space; we can call a town or woods a particular space. But what do we recognise in those spaces? The awareness of space changes with one's intentionality. Sometimes we can think of the space inside a bottle as a particular place.

We find the 'field' through our intentionality. It's the same in my field recording. This new work requires two people: two people make one stereo sound image. It's a crazy experiment to construct a stereo image, like making a clapping sound with two hands. We capture one image with two inputs, which is normally what our eyes and ears do.

CC: Doesn't every microphone manifest this intentionality? We choose to point it in this or that direction. Why place the stethoscope microphones on someone's temples? Are you trying to draw attention to the subjectivity of auditory experience? And is 'objectivity' defined by a multiplication of subjective experiences?

TS: The body is not the important thing here. What's important is turning the focus onto something. Mics can be attached to any part of the body, but the temple is the suitable part for me. Simply pointing a microphone is not satisfactory for me.

And, yes, I am trying to call attention to the subjectivity of the listener. I know it's difficult to express a subjective experience in art. My subjective experience is not shared by the listener. The object I choose is not related to the listener because it is dictated by my own interests. Two people face something (an object), and there is intentionality and subjective experience. Hopefully, when a listener listens to (or sees) my recording, he or she will understand it represents the intentionality and subjective experience of two people. With the stethoscope attached, we record the intentional state of facing an object. On the recording, two people each form an arrow towards the object. The two do not compare their subjective experience or their intentionality; but they are performing the same action during the recording. These two inputs (and outputs) make a stereo image.

With regard to objectivity, the philosopher Thomas Nagel said one's death is quite different from others'. 'Objectivity' means believing that two persons who do the same action might have the same viewpoint together. A Temple Recording makes a landscape image as their experience. The aim of this work is difficult to explain and to understand because it comprises not only a hearing work but also a recording work. It is searching for another possible relationship between oneself and an object (or the world). I recently had a big surprise (maybe this is confusing for logical people): I got up in the morning, opened the window and heard the ambience in the distance. It's nothing special. In fact it's very common and usual. But I found that the sound had very similar acoustics to the Temple Recording. Then I started to think about the meaning of the word 'ambience'. Anyway, I think that the sound of the Temple Recording is interesting in itself without my concept or information. But I don't want listeners to hear it without my concept or information because I am not a musician.

CC: In the third part of *A Grammar for Listening,* Luke Fowler filmed several of your Temple Recordings. What can the filmic image add to this project?

TS: The Temple Recording is difficult to understand through sound alone. The listener isn't privy to the situation of the recording. So I do want him or her to have access to this situation (that is, two people place microphones on their temples and face a landscape).

LAURA GANNON WITH
MINA BANCHEVA

THE HOUSE WITH A
FIXED EYE

INTRODUCTION
Laura Gannon

Drawing is something I've always done, but rarely exhibited. I am increasingly conscious of my methods of production and my focus, until now, has been primarily my film work. Recently, I've been examining my drawings and question their role in relation to filmmaking and my practice as a whole.

My drawings are quickly made, usually in series, and produced from a psychological perspective informed by unconscious drives and desires, rather than references to external objects or situations. My films, by contrast, are made over a long period of time, involving fundraising and working with a crew. Thus, the immediacy of the drawings don't necessarily translate into the films.

I invited Mina Bancheva, a psychotherapist, to discuss my drawings and examine the unconscious motives at work in my practice. The drawings relate to remembering one person from my life, and using that figure as a point of departure to create a stage and a setting within which that person (or versions of that person) performs.

The size and fragility of the drawings make me feel vulnerable. Unlike film, the small scale presents a more intimate method of viewing. Working with Mina helps me understand and recognise the language contained within the drawings. Through this recognition, the films may re-emerge as a parallel language that, together with the drawings, might constitute a practice.

Mina and I also examine *World/Interior* (2010), a film set in an empty house. The building possesses human characteristics: it can hear and observe what happens within its walls. In some ways, the house is a stage-set: characters enter, collide, interact, perform and leave. The camera is a visitor in a site where the action has already taken place. But this house is not a home; it does not offer homecoming. A second film is referenced in our discussions: *her grace o'malice*, my film proposal based on an historical figure Grace O'Malley, a sixteenth-century pirate from the West of Ireland.

MY THERAPEUTIC FRAME OF WORK
Mina Bancheva

My therapeutic frame of work has its base in Cognitive Analytical
Therapy (CAT). CAT integrates two main therapeutic perspectives:
first, the psychoanalytical/psychodynamic stance; second, the
principles of change as advocated by the cognitive behaviour
therapies. CAT differs from both modalities in that it puts strong
emphasis on relationships (including the relationships between
client and therapist), thus allowing meaning to be constructed in
dialogue with the client.

CAT postulates that as human beings we develop in relation to
significant others in our lives and that we also learn who we are in
the context of these relationships. In my work, although I spend
some time exploring the past relational experiences of my clients,
I tend to focus on the here and now, both of my client's life and
of the therapeutic hour and I rarely offer one-sided analytical
interpretations. I work in dialogue with my client to understand
where they are coming from and help them make sense of their
experiences both in the past and now.

Despite the fact that my work is informed by the basic psycho-
analytical/psychodynamic theories of development, my aim is to
guide clients and to encourage them to become autonomous agents
in the creation of new paradigms of understanding, insight and
behaviour.

LITERARY ADDENDUM TO WORLD / INTERIOR
Laura Gannon

Round the curtained bedhead, Pompeian red walls drank objects into their shadow: picture frames, armies of bottles, boxes, an ornate clock showed without glinting, as though not quite painted out by some dark transparent wash.

Downstairs was a photograph of the house as it used to be, in winter, a grey façade of light-reflecting windows, flanked each side by groves of skeleton trees. In the sun, the curtains were flame-pink; prismatic crystal candlesticks shot rays out; the flooded empty white room looked like a stage. 'Home' was always downstairs; downstairs is always safe. Upstairs is crazy with dreams or love. The window was open behind the curtains and the hot night air came in. The telephone held her eye; she saw it was going to speak. A yellow rose on the mantlepiece suddenly shed its petals, but it did not make her start. Karen did not go out that day; she did not dare take her eyes off the house. Sun on the hall floor, steps upstairs in the house had this same deadly intention not to know.

She would have heard everything. You know our hall is dark and she wears black; I only saw her face, which seemed to be hanging there. When he opened the door she smiled and came in calmly, with the quiet manner she has when there is no more to know. After that it was strange that I heard no movement anywhere in the house. I did not know what I feared. I began to go down. Our street door was wide open and three or four people stood out there in the daylight, staring at our doorstep.

The room is not light, and till then I had looked only at her. But then I saw his blood splashed in the marble, on the parquet where he stood and in a trail to the door, smeared where I had trodden without knowing. When she could not speak, Leopold turned round facing the mantlepiece and suddenly ground his forehead against the marble. Karen was no longer compelling the house with her eye: the house with its fixed eye was compelling Karen.

Selected extracts from Elizabeth Bowen, *The House in Paris*, 1935

WORLD / INTERIOR: AN ANALYSIS
Mina Bancheva

In the film *World/Interior*, the house sees itself through the eye of the camera. Mirror compositions appear throughout the film, playing with light and reflection. Ordinary life goes on but this is not reflected in the eye of the camera, like looking in a mirror and seeing no reflection.

The film depicts neglect and decay: crumbling walls are patterned by mould, and the house holds shabby furniture, musty books, a dirt-encrusted toaster, pills abandoned on an empty shelf. There are old bird feathers on a mantlepiece and bird shit splatters the back of the sofa; life has entered the house from the outside only to perish. The old house was once gracious, gilded frames surrounding scenes of worship and devotion, accompanied by elegant music that carries the echoes of a bygone era.

But the past is now trapped by the present: the plain mirror, the carriage clock, the toaster and the plastic kettle, the green felt pen. These objects lie in crude juxtaposition to what once was loved and cherished.

It is difficult to know what the artist feels this. It is as if the objectivity of her camera serves to conceal the inner emotional connection to the object (the house) under surveillance. There is a sense of things laid bare but to what avail? The artist seems impartial to beauty or decay, seemingly non-judgemental of what she presents to us.

The film is a revelation of the power of objects to tell a story. The crockery, the books, the furniture, some covered, some left bare made me think of the house as a place in transition, a house waiting for something, or somebody to make a decision about its fate. Will the house be restored to its former self or will someone new come along and take it into the new century?

As it is now, I am left with the cameo shot of an armchair by the window in the room with blue walls. Looking out into the street, the house opposite is reflected back in the window. This shot has the quality of a painting, as if the absence of the person who once sat there sums up the underlying melancholy of the house.

AN EXCHANGE

Laura Gannon and Mina Bancheva

MINA BANCHEVA: There is a huge difference between talking about the work with the artist and writing about it at a distance. In the first instance, by talking about it together, we create meaning between us through the experience of interacting. So, writing about it without you allows me to create a unilateral interpretation. This is not how I work in therapy; our work together has been totally interactive. I check meaning with you every step of the way to ensure that we make sense of it together.

When I was writing about your work on my own, all I could do was express the impact it had on me, which is very different from talking with you and asking you what you had in mind when you were doing it.

I was struck by the fact that the camera was so impartial, I wanted to check with you what that was like for you. There is a withholding there. It's as if you and the house featured in the film can't quite make up its mind which life to live: the old one or the new one.

LAURA GANNON: The way I work is naturally quite sparse. It is not the language of Minimalism, but I don't put create a fiction of the work either.

MB: Some images that come to mind appear to tease the viewer, which can be called 'withholding'. Why are you doing this, for example, by leaving some objects uncovered while others remain covered? You just show bits, and you leave the rest up to the viewer. How much of 'you' was actually in the film?

LG: The film works on two levels. The camera looks at the architectural parts of every room, working with the idea of a walk-through and thinking about what you take in when you see the space. The visuals tell a story. I use sound to create a spatial environment. In an empty house, the sounds are very different to those you hear when you walk into a house that contains other people. I used immediate sounds, such as the radio, to heighten the sense of sound in the film.

MB: It was impossible for me to look at the film and not make up a story about it, like the scene where you show a hanging dress—as a viewer, you can make a story. I wanted to respond in the prose poem I sent to you previously:

> *'Someone plays the piano*
> *And a white dress hangs over a door frame*
> *Are these echoes and imprints*
> *Of old ghosts or the living…'*

LG: The sounds of people who lived there—

MB:—that's how I understood the film. The viewer is able make up a story.

LG: That's the nature of looking at art—you're coming with your own images and memories. For some, this relates to the house depicted in the film, while for other people the space would have no reference.

MB: Lets have a look at the drawings; you brought those five together.

LG: They were done as a set.

MB: They seem to be the outcome of an internal battle.

DRAWING NO. 1

MB: Can you describe this to me?

LG: The large animal is in control. She is powerful and occupies most of the space. It is a stage setting complete with curtain in right corner.

MB: Yes, it looks feminine. It looks as if the creature's toenails are painted. She appears very comfortable with her power, regal in her posture and stance but with a rather contemptuous air: she is in repose but vigilant, as if ready to pounce.

LG: The smaller animal is calculated in its expression, diminished and unhappy. It has to be content with a small bowl of food. It is angry at the strength and position of the larger animal, who seems to be dominating the situation. The smaller animal is at the edge of the page.

MB: Yes, it's sneaking into the picture. It looks scheming and

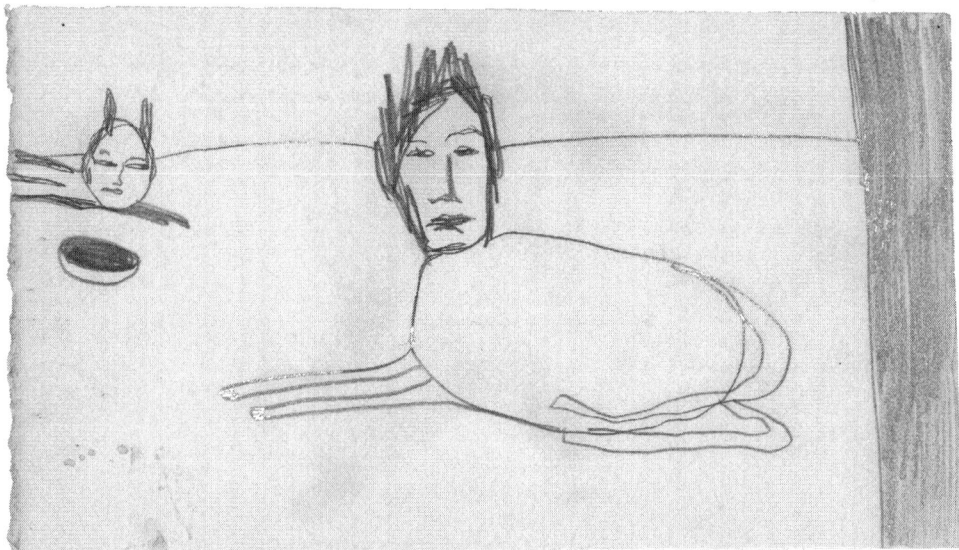

spiteful, as if it is biding its time, listening and waiting for the right time to come to sneak in and snatch what it wants. The second part of the picture may be a warning of what may happen if it tries to vie for power with the larger animal; it may get flattened by the stronger, more dominant power of the larger animal.

LG: I was thinking of a particular person when I made the drawing. She held position of power within the family dynamic all her adult life. This power was used in a bullying manner to control those who were dependent on her. It is not a balanced use of power. It's power at the expense of diminishing others.

MB: That's interesting. One analytical interpretation of the picture could be that the large animal represents the super-ego, and the small one stands for the ego. If we relate this to the psychology of the individual (to you, the artist), it may represent the painful split between the fantasy of power and grandeur, coupled with a contemptuous inner position on the one hand and the part that feels inferior, contemptible and lacking in status and power. The powerless part could represent the 'child' part of the individual, who feels manipulated and controlled by the dominant and demanding adult figure. The former finds a way of surviving and acquiring power by behaving in scheming and sneaky ways to get what it wants. But it can be easily flattened and diminished by the expectations of internalised parental demands. I find this picture disturbing in what I perceived it to be: a representation of the painful dynamics of the wounded part of an individual's psyche.

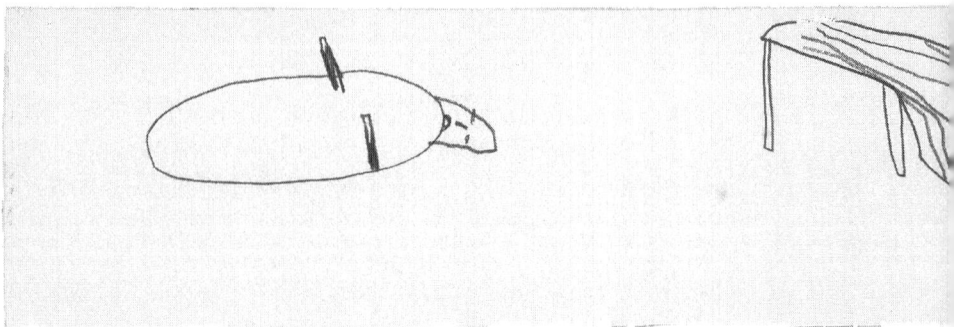

DRAWING NO. 2

LG: Here is a table with legs. Fabric is draped over the table.

MB: I see these as Japanese shoes, you know, those shoes with the big wooden heels. Also I see a connection between *Drawing no. 1* and *Drawing no. 2*. My interpretation of the drawings is this: it's the battle of the super-ego and the ego.

LG: I was thinking of my grandmother when doing *Drawing no. 1*.

MB: It is also what's internalised by you: the not good-enough, flattened by the heel in *Drawing no. 2*.

LG: And angry to be in that position.

MB: The strip below the main picture in *Drawing no. 2* is also interesting. A small animal lies flattened, paws up in the air, looking totally helpless and powerless. Perhaps this is the price to pay for trying to 'sneak in' on the superior, queenly power of the super-ego.

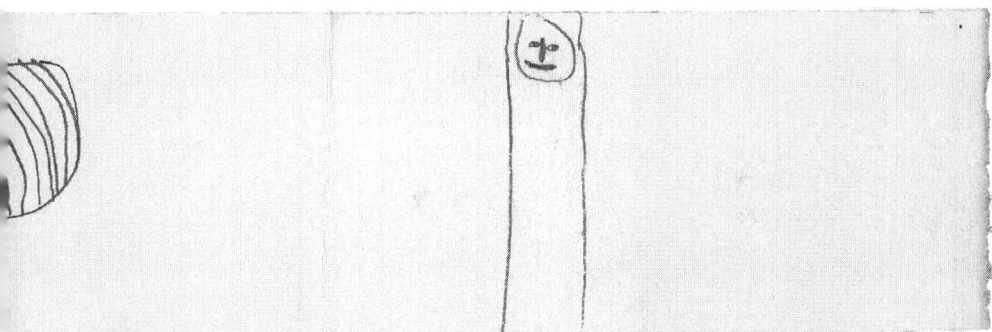

DRAWING NO. 3

LG: I drew this in response to visiting my grandmother. She was constantly rubbing her hands on a blanket when she talked to me, as if she was trying to heal a trauma that my mother and I were unaware of.

MB: There is a lot of pain when you look at it. Her energy is dormant.

LG: Because of the amount of grief that she had experienced she was prone to unpredictable behaviour, but she also had a dazzling personality that would seduce everyone around her.

MB: You made this when your grandmother was in hospital. She seems to be sleeping, completely peaceful.

DRAWING NO. 4

LG: There is a book in this image.

MB: What is the meaning of a book for you?

LG: You can let the pages open into different sculptural shapes. Books are very tangible objects.

MB: There is something here about security.

LG: Yes.

MB: The house in your film *World/Interior* featured a lot of books.

LG: I have always enjoyed books as objects, beyond what is contained within them.

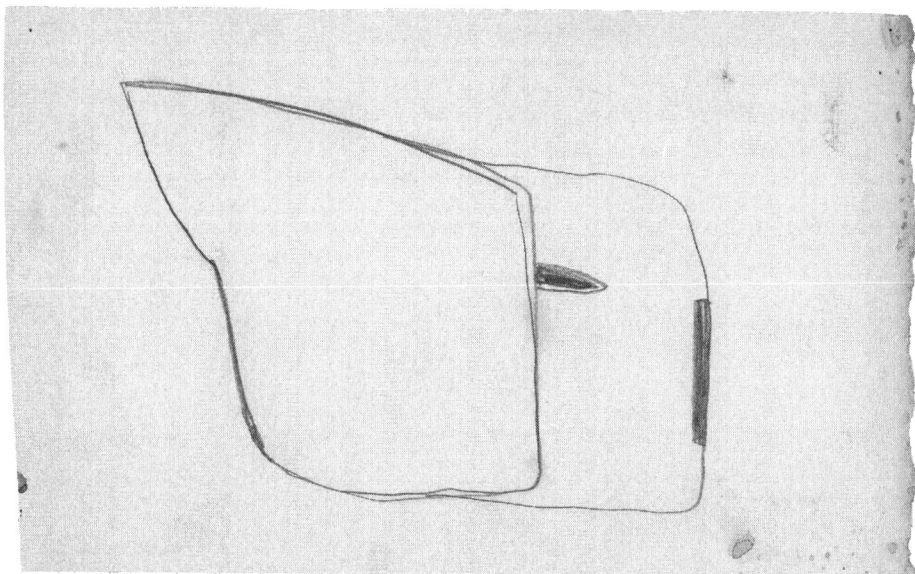

DRAWING NO. 5

MB: And this one?

LG: It's a leaf instead of the mouth.

MB: What kind of a leaf?

LG: One part of something.

MB: It's not unique. New energy, isn't it?

LG: New energy?

MB: These objects have different meaning to different people. The mouth and the eyes... there's something you wanted in the mouth and the eyes.

LG: There is some similarity between the face in this drawing and the face in *Drawing no. 1*: both depict a figure looking out from the corner of their eyes. And yet the eyes in *Drawing no. 1* are more calculated; here they are more relaxed and benign.

MB: It's more optimistic.

LG: The drawings work as a suite of drawings rather than individual works. *Drawing no. 1* shows the stage and the curtain; the rest are what happens on that stage.

MB: My interpretation is coloured by what I know about you, as opposed to actually having a conversation that make sense of sense of something between us. I don't want to expose of you. Sometimes therapists write about their cases, and I'm aware that I have got your permission to do that.

WORK IN PROGRESS: *HER GRACE O'MALICE*

MB: I think there's a link between the large queenly figure or animal in *Drawing no. 1* and the protagonist in your proposed film *her grace o'malice*.

LG: The figure in *Drawing no. 1* represents power. Grace O'Malley was a sixteenth-century Irish pirate who visited Elizabeth I and petitioned the Queen for concessions, including the right to continue sailing, a widow's pension and the release of her imprisoned son. I'm interested in the giving and taking of power between two women, and this does perhaps link *Drawing no. 1* to the film, except the second smaller figure in the drawing is clearly no match for the large figure.

MB: What motivated you to choose this particular story? Do you identify with the qualities that you set out to portray in the film?

LG: Grace is a strategist at work; she got results from taking on an absolute power. I am not comparing my personality to hers, but I am interested in a woman who is from the same geographical location as me. I'm familiar with the culture and history that she came from.

MB: She had boldness, an ability to put her neck on the line.

LG: She was a risk taker; she had the courage to be a gambler.

LG: The small animal in *Drawing no. 1* is never going to do that.

MB: The film shifts the position of power. Grace was very aware of her own power, and didn't take on the Queen from a position of subordination.

LG: She belonged the last generation who had their power base outside the empire.

MB: What do you mean by this?

LG: Until the late sixteenth century, the West of Ireland was ruled by local chiefs who were heads of an extended family, a 'clan'. The ownership of land and property belonged to the clan, not an individual leader. When British rule reached the West of Ireland, agents for the crown promoted primogeniture, which wasn't part of Celtic customs and laws. Grace's family was a clan and in her lifetime clans gave up their Celtic title in exchange for a British one with protection from the Crown. The school history that I learned in the West of Ireland was one a history of subordination—of famine, economic failure and continuous battles with the coloniser.

MB: Grace O'Malley was left out of the history books.

LG: There were few female examples. The protagonists and makers of history were men. Grace was part of folklore and women were generally relegated to the sidelines.

MB: In *Drawing no. 1*, the power is centre stage, the little animal is in the sidelines. Does the film attempts to readdress this? It is as if the film is saying it doesn't have to be like this, that women are in full possession of power.

LG: Grace operated outside a system. Her power was taken and, for the most part, her activities were illegal.

MB: She broke the rules. What about the relationship between the two queens?

LG: In the film you don't see the meeting between her and Queen Elizabeth. Everything is conveyed from Grace's perspective.

MB: Giving her a voice.

LG: I'm attempting to humanise a mythological figure by presenting her as an older woman striving to improve her situation. I haven't included Queen Elizabeth as she is so frequently portrayed in film and history and is therefore already defined and characterised.

MB: Elizabeth's power was inherited, whereas Grace became a pirate—she chose to live a masculine life.

LG: Both women took on masculine roles.

MB: An artist's choice of subject matter comes from the unconscious mind. By choosing Grace as your subject, I think your unconscious mind is at work. Grace could have failed, but she took the risk and didn't.

DUNCAN MARQUISS
WITH LARS BANG LARSEN

VOLLEY

To be mad with lucidity and in complete possession of one's intellectual faculties — this, surely must be one of the most terrible of experiences. Unimpaired, Surin's reason looked on helplessly, while his imagination, his emotions and his autonomic nervous system comported themselves like an alliance of criminal maniacs, bent on his destruction. It was a struggle, in the last analysis, between the active person and the victim of suggestion.

— Aldous Huxley, *The Devils of Loudun*, 1952

If I dream about someone, ask that person a question, I won't know what that person has said until he has said it. Yet that someone is a product of my brain, a brief and momentary extension of it.

— Stanislaw Lem, *Tales of Pirx the Pilot*, 1979

We think of ourselves as Knights of the Holy Contact. This is another lie. We are only seeking Man. We have no need of other worlds. We need mirrors.

— Stanislaw Lem, *Solaris*, 1961

The black paper between a mirror
Breaks my heart that I can't go
Steal softly thru sunshine
Steal softly through snow

— Captain Beefheart, 'Steal Softly Thru Snow', *Trout Mask Replica*, 1969

The mind lets in the light, then the dark, in interaction; so time is generated.

— Philip K. Dick, *Valis*, 1981

Suddenly, in lithe and terrible silence, with dancer's grace, three figures, long-limbed, effeminate, dressed in black tights, leotards and gloves, black silk hose pulled over their faces, come capering on stage and stop, gazing at him. Their faces behind the stockings are shadowy and deformed. They wait. The lights all go out.

— Thomas Pynchon, *The Crying of Lot 49*, 1965

As she talked she began to disappear. He watched her go; it was amazing. Gloria in her measured way, talked herself out of existence word by word. It was rationality at the service of — well, he thought, at the service of nonbeing. Her mind had become one great, expert eraser.

— Philip K Dick, *op. cit*

The painter isolates his subject, which is the first way of unifying it. Landscapes flee, vanish from the memory, or destroy one another.

— Albert Camus, *The Rebel,* 1951

The Corn-spirit as a Wolf or a Dog. Thus, when the wind sets the corn in wave-like motion the peasants often say, "the Wolf is going over, or through, the corn", "the Rye-wolf is rushing over the field", "the wolf is in the corn".

— James Frazer, *The Golden Bough,* 1922

Satan is the yeast of the universe.

— Alexander Scriabin in Leonid Sabaneyev, *Vospominaniya o Skriabine,* 1925

Affect is the site of alienation. It is in affect that alienation is generated. The experience of the surrounding world replaces the materiality of the surrounding world, and becomes a place for the production of the nausea and of those fantasies that constitute the ontology of the alienated subject. It is a condition that thus stands in an incomprehensible and indirect relation to the surrounding world, in that its basis is the affectation's space of effects, rather than the causality of affect. The surrounding world is treated in a similarly indirect manner by the alienated subject, whose acts are speculative, fabulating or paranoid. In this sense the alienated subject is paralysed. Apathetic. Incapable of direct action. Incapable of understanding The Common Good, that in an evil logic often becomes the concept that haunts the alienated subject, and that this enlightened and free human being probably has enlarged himself in a massive way. Of course.

— Søren Andreasen, 'Den ligeglade: Angsten for ikke at kunne begribe Det Almene', Andreasen and Schmidt-Rasmussen, *New Age,* trans. Lars Bang Larsen

After a while he asked, "What is I?"
She grinned. "First of all it's very important. A good deal more important
than anything else. The brain will let any number of things go to pot as
long as 'I' stay alive. That's because the brain is part of I. A book is, a ship is,
Jebel is, the universe is, but, as you must have noticed, I am."
The Butcher nodded. "Yes. But I am what?"

— Samuel R Delany, *Babel-17*, 1966

One is always half mad when one is shy of people.

— Robert Walser, *Jakob von Gunten*, 1909

I could dwell a great while upon the calamities of this dreadful time, and
go on to describe the objects that appeared among us every day, the dreadful
extravagancies which the distraction of sick people drove them into; how
the streets began now to be fuller of frightful objects, and families to be
made even a terror to themselves. But after I have told you, as I have above,
that one man, being tied in his bed, and finding no other way to deliver
himself, set the bed on fire with his candle, which unhappily stood within
his reach, and burnt himself in his bed and how another, by the insufferable
torment he bore, danced and sung naked in the streets, not knowing one
ecstasy from another; I say, after I have mentioned these things, what can
be added more? What can be said to represent the misery of these times
more lively to the reader, or to give him a more perfect idea of complicated
distress?

— Daniel Defoe, *A Journal of a Plague Year*, 1722

The comet roared with its flaming tail right through the valley, across the
forest and the mountains, and then disappeared again over the edge of the
world. If it had come a tiny bit nearer to the earth I am quite sure that none
of us would be here now. But it just gave a whisk of its tail and swept off to
another solar system far away, and it has never been seen since.
But in the cave they didn't know all this. He thought everything had been
burnt up or smashed to atoms when the comet came down, and that their
cave was the only thing left in the whole world. They listened and listened,
but all they heard was silence.

— Tove Jansson, *Comet in Moominland*, 1959

The infinite arrives barefoot on this earth.

— Hans Arp, as quoted in Christopher Middleton's introduction to Robert Walser, *Jakob von Gunten*

I cannot say, as some do, this Devil is not so black, as he is painted; for indeed no colours can represent the Place to the Life, nor any Soul conceive aright of it, but those who have been Sufferers there: but how Hell should become by degrees so natural, and not only tolerable, but even agreeable, is a thing Unintelligible, but by those who have Experienc'd it, as I have.

— Daniel Defoe, *Moll Flanders*, 1722

What is more arrogant than honesty?

— Ursula K Le Guin, *The Left Hand of Darkness*, 1969

Going to the cinema results in an immobilisation of the body. Not much gets in the way of one's perception. All one can do is look and listen. One forgets where one is sitting ... Does it matter what film one is watching?

— Robert Smithson, *A Cinematic Atopia*, 1971

We know of primitive peoples of the so-called pre-animistic stage who identify themselves with sacred animals and plants and name themselves after them; we know of insane people who likewise identify themselves in part with objects of their perception, which are thus no longer objecta, 'placed before' them.

— Walter Benjamin, *On the Program of the Coming Philosophy*, 1918

A butterfly, in order to make itself invisible, may do nothing more than use the tactics of the Satyride Asiatique, whose flattened wings in repose appear simply as a line almost without thickness, imperceptible, perpendicular to the flower where it has alighted, and which turns simultaneously with the observer so that it is only this minimum surface that is always seen.

— Roger Callios, *Mimicry and Legendary Psychasthenia*, 1935

Among distinctions, there is assuredly none more clear-cut than that between the organism and its surroundings ... The invariable response of schizophrenics to the question: where are you? I know where I am, but I do not feel as though I'm at the spot where I find myself. To these dispossessed souls, space seems to be a devouring force.

— Roger Callios, *ibid*.

Have you seen a butterfly round a candle? That's how he will keep circling and circling round me. Freedom will lose its attractions. He'll begin to brood, he'll weave a tangle round himself, he'll worry himself to death! What's more he will provide me with a mathematical proof — if I only give him long enough interval...And he'll keep circling round me, getting nearer and nearer and then — flop! He'll fly straight into my mouth and I'll swallow him, and that will be very amusing, he-he-he!

— Fyodor Dostoyevsky, *Crime and Punishment*, 1866

The sprouting stops. Night. Localised death. No more desire, no more appetite, for talking.

— Henri Michaux, *Darkness Moves: an Henri Michaux Anthology*, 1927–1984

On the blackboard and in our notebooks we write: colour is the most relative medium in art.

— Josef Albers, *Interaction of Colour*, 1963

Why colour causes reality to tilt remains a mystery.

— Michale Taussig, *My Cocaine Museum*, 2004

Everybody knows that "pathetic" colours don't exist.

— Robert Smithson, *Incidents of Mirror-Travel in the Yucatan*, 1969

From the remote depths of the corridor, the mirror spied upon us.
We discovered (such a discovery is inevitable in the late hours of the night)
that mirrors have something monstrous about them. Then Bioy Casares
recalled that one of the heresiarchs of Uqbar had declared that mirrors and
copulation are abominable because they increase the number of men.

— Jorge Louis Borges, 'Tlon, Uqbar, Orbis Tertius', 1940

Once you start seeing objects in a positive or negative way you are on the
road to derangement.

— Robert Smithson, *op cit.*

He lives in a state of pure contradiction between two urges; one for
destruction, the other for order. The outcome is a form of delirium ...

— Denis Duclos, *The Werewolf Complex,* 1998

The Roggenwolf ('rye-wolf') of German rural folklore is a demon that lives
in grainfields and ambushes peasants, strangling them. This creature,
essentially a type of werewolf, is represented at harvest-time by the last
sheaf, which is called 'Wolf' and tied up to nullify its malignance ... Another
lupine connection is the fungus ergot, which is particularly associated with
Rye, is sometimes known as Wolf or Wolfszahn ('Wolf-tooth').
Ergot contains a number of interesting substances, chief among which is
lysergic acid, from which the hallucinogen LSD is made ... the symptoms of
ergotism mimic lycanthropic behaviour.

— Alby Stone, *Hellhounds, Werewolves and the Germanic Underworld,* 1994

The future of our struggle is the future of fear, FEAR!! The fear of free
love, fear of not working, fear of youth ... We drink the magic potion and
become the spectre that haunts Amerika. We are the WEREWOLVES
baying at
the moon and tearing at the fat. Fangs sharpened, claws dripping. We are
not afraid. We create fear. (The Pig wanders from his sty ... and the wolves
descend). "Where do they come from?" Who knows. "What do they want?"
They won't say. But the moon knows. And the WEREWOLVES know.
And the fat frightened giant gulps tranquilisers while his children grow hair
and fangs and leave home to run with the wolves.
The worst fear is the fear of the unknown, and we are the unknown ...
THE UNKNOWN ...
WE ARE WEREWOLVES!
International Werewolf Conspiracy
Up Against the Wall / Motherfuckers

— Up Against the Wall Motherfucker, *A Motherfucker is a Werewolf,* 1968

A pungent smell of vegetation welled up and filled Sasha's empty head as
though someone had suddenly pumped a jet of gas into a balloon. The
balloon grew and stretched, straining upwards with ever greater force until
suddenly it broke the slim thread binding it to the earth and soared
upwards — leaving the forest and the clearing with the fire and the people far
below, and the scattered clouds came rushing towards him, followed by the
stars.

— Victor Pelevin, *A Werewolf Problem in Central Russia and
Other Stories,* 1998

But this will feel like a record of the last wilderness on earth, a film to be
taken into outer space as a souvenir of what nature once was. I want to
convey a feeling of absolute aloneness, a kind of Goodbye to Earth which
I believe we are living through ... It will preserve what will increasingly
become an extreme rarity: wilderness. Perhaps aloneness will also become
a rarity.

— Michael Snow, *Proposal to the Canadian Film Development
Corporation,* 1969

You vary yourself according to the wavelength. You change your shape, your volume, your colour, and you then belong so completely to the space, that the flat lived in me just as much as I did in it.

— Marie Darrieussecq, *Ghost Flat (A Modern Couple)*, 2005

Architectural space overwhelms me. To paint a picture on a surface or to make a sculpture is so different from living in architectural terms! Now, I am no longer alone. I am pumped up by others. Perception so powerful that I feel myself torn up from my roots. Unstable in space. I feel as though I were in the process of disintegrating. To live perception, to be perception ... Often I awaken before the window of my room — looking for the exterior space as though it were "inside". I am afraid of space — but I reconstruct myself by means of it. During crises, it escapes me. It's as though we played — myself and it — at cat and mouse, at winner loses.

— Lygia Clark, '1965: About the Act', 1965

All these consequences are implied in the statement that the worker is related to the product of labour as to an alien object. For on this premise it is clear that the more the worker spends himself, the more powerful becomes the alien world of objects which he creates over and against himself, the poorer he himself — his inner world — becomes, the less belongs to him as his own. It is the same in religion. The more man puts into God, the less he retains in himself. The worker puts his life into the object; but now his life no longer belongs to him but to the object. Thence, the greater this activity, the more the worker lacks objects. Whatever the product of his labour is, he is not. Therefore, the greater this product, the less is he himself. The alienation of the worker in his product means not only that his labour becomes an object, an external existence, but that it exists outside him, independently, as something alien to him, and that it becomes a power on its own confronting him. It means that the life which he has conferred on the object confronts him as something hostile and alien.

— Karl Marx, *Economic and Philosophical Manuscripts of 1844*

OM VAJRA BHÛMI ÂH HÛM
The base transforms into a powerful ground of gold
OM VAJRA REKHE ÂH HÛM
The outer periphery becomes a jeweled fence of iron mountains
The Great Liberation by Hearing in the Intermediate States
(also titled *The Tibetan Book of the Dead*)
Amongst Mahometans, the following legend is said to be accepted as
an account of the miraculous introduction of the "wond'rous weed"
to the world.

Mahomet, passing the desert in winter, found a poor viper frozen on the
ground; touched with compassion, he placed it in his sleeve, where the warmth
and glow of the blessed body restored it to life. No sooner did the ungrateful
reptile find its health restored, than it poked forth its head and said —
　　"Oh, Prophet, I am going to bite you."
　　"Give me a sound reason, O snake, and I will be content."
　　"Your people kill my people constantly, there is war between your race
　　and mine."
　　"Your people bite my people, the balance between our kindred is even,
　　between you and me; nay, it is in my favour, for I have done you good."
　　"And that you may not do me harm, I will bite you."
　　"Do not be so ungrateful."
　　"I will! I have sworn by the Most High that I will."
At the Name the Prophet no longer opposed the viper, but bade him bite
on, in the name of God. The snake pierced his fangs in the blessed wrist,
which the Prophet not liking, shook him off, but did him no further harm,
nor would he suffer those near him to destroy it, but putting his lips to the
wound, and sucking out the poison, spat it upon the earth. From these drops
sprang that wond'rous weed, which has the bitterness of the serpent's
quelled by the sweet saliva of the Prophet.

Happy Moslem! You have solved the mystery, and your heart feels no doubt;
but Christian dogs despairingly sigh for some revelation from the past,
whether through history or tradition, of the first use of this plant.

— Mordecai Cooke, *The Seven Sisters of Sleep*, 1860

It should be understood that this radiating vibration [of thought] conveys the character of the thought, but not its subject. If a Hindu sits rapt in devotion to Krishna, the waves of feeling which pour forth from him stimulate devotional feeling in all those who come under their influence, though in the case of the Muhammadan that devotion is to Allah, while for the Zoroastrian it is to Ahuramazda, or for the Christian to Jesus. A man thinking keenly upon some high subject pours out from himself vibrations which tend to stir up thought at a similar level in others, but they in no way suggest to those others the special subject of his thought.

— Annie Besant and Charles W Leadbeater, *Thought-Forms,* 1901

We have been very strenuously conditioned against solitude. To be alone is considered to be a grievous and dangerous condition.

— Agnes Martin, *Writings,* 1991

When a predator is stalking a shoal of minnows (Phoxinus phoxinus), guppies (Poecilia reticulata) or sticklebacks (Gasterosteus aculeatus), individuals will separate from the shoal, swim tentatively towards the predator until only a few body lengths away, wait there for a few seconds and then slowly return to the shoal. It has been suggested that in such visits the fish can gather information about the identity, precise location and current motivational state of the predator.

— M Milinski and TCM Bakker, 'Female sticklebacks use male colouration in mate choice and hence avoid parasitised males', *Nature,* 1990

There is no up or down
Your truth is the only master
Death is made by the living
Pain is only intense to you
The sun shines every day
Freedom Freedom

— Flower Travellin' Band, *Satori,* 1970

LAURE PROUVOST

THE POLICEMAN,
THE IRONMONGER,
THE NEUROSCIENTIST,
THE PRIEST,
THE SHOPKEEPER,
THE PSYCHOANALYST,
THE GHOSTWRITER
AND
THE BUTCHER'S WIFE

INTRODUCTION
Laure Prouvost

This is about commissioning and interpretation. I commissioned eight people who each work within a specific profession to respond to one of my videos, IT, HEAT, HIT (2010). This six-minute video piece is usually presented as a large projection work, but in this instance I was interested in the different contexts and understanding of the work, involving people with different interests and paths in life. I didn't want a single response, or even a dialogue, but instead an extended and complex (mis)understanding of the work.

Showing this video in different environments was quite magical. In the workshop of the ironmonger, the machines stopped and his attention was on the film playing on my laptop. The environment gave the film another narrative. I asked him what he thought about the film and how he would like to respond. First, he suggested he would make a tray for me (because that is what he is good at doing). I asked him if he could maybe respond more to the film. He then said he could make a tree. I said that this was fine if that was what the film made him feel. Then he then said, "I could make you a tree in a tray". I said "perfect". When I went to collect his work, he had made a tree, but not in a tray. He said it was not holding well in a tray. The butcher's wife wrote a complimentary short note; she had to be careful not to loose a good customer. That's professional.

I want to explore what might organise our creativity and our responses, as well as understand how we consider what is valuable and important. A work is always understood through one's interpretation and where one mind is at; it's about losing control, being out of sync, even when just hinting possibilities.

POLICEMAN
Hakim Sadouk

Passion, love and violence are all portrayed in It, Heat, Hit. As a police officer, what springs to mind when watching this video is how close and yet different these three words can be. The photos and the video sequences take you from one dimension to another in an instant. The film moves from peaceful and calming photos, to sexy scenes, then to violent and abstract photos, all while playing a well-adapted and executed music track accompanied by the soft voice of the narrator. This is the type of pattern one sees over and over again in a domestic incident: love is followed by violence, then immediately by passion, but not always in this sequence.

The image that sticks most in my mind is the carrot being chopped in half. It is a powerful statement that expresses the amount of passion needed to commit any act of extreme violence. In this instance, it took a fraction of a second to commit the act, but maybe a long time to plan and certainly a much longer time to fix. This is the way crime is committed. The point of no return is what this act is about — the point at which reflection takes control, and not in a positive way.

IRONMONGER
Hikmet Savci

I liked the film. When I watched the flames I felt comfortable. It felt relaxing, like I was paralysed. The story is like a new galaxy, a new world, with nice sound and picture. It was a very good designer who put it together. When you're talking, you are taking people inside, you're listening to everything. You take the inside of the people. I can watch stories like this any time.

I think it would be good to show this film to everyone. It would be good to see it in the cinema, like an action movie. When I first saw the film, I saw flames, the seaside, people, a tray, water. Afterwards, I thought that you needed a different type of design, something Victorian, something old-fashioned, so I made the tray from metal, by hand.

NEUROSCIENTIST
Dr H Anne Leaver

Perception and Association of Visual Information in the Imagery of IT, HEAT, HIT by Laure Prouvost

S u m m a r y : The video installation IT, HEAT, HIT presents a series of visual images, accompanied by auditory and textual commentary, in a loose narrative. The perception of reality and experience is questioned, and the closest reality appears to be the response of the viewer to the video's images, either directly and readily interpreted, like 'heat' associated with the colour red, 'pain', associated with jagged images, or the examples of 'hit' starting with amputation of the viewer's leg, to the more elusive 'it', possibly associated with calm and the cool pleasurable images which predominate in the initial sections of the narrative.
A i m s : The question of reality and perception is raised at the beginning and the end of the narrative and at several stages during the sequence, for example the suggestion of rejection (eating the image). The narrative aims to suggest a series of experiences, including calm, confusion, disorientation, rejection, anger, and jealousy. There appears to be an association of colours, (for example blue, white and red), with mood, and of shapes with perception and experience (angles, edges, knives, needles, broken glass, pneumatic drill, smoke, compared with apple, trees, stone, feather, swimming frog, eggs, leaves, snow).

Structure: The viewer is invited to enter the narrative, stating that the individuals will not exist unless the viewer allows them to do so, by viewing the video sequence. It states that the viewer can terminate this existence by exiting after six minutes. However, this is the length of the full video, at which stage the viewer is asked to leave, suggesting that the narrative is also able to influence the observer. The sequence begins with calm aquatic summer images, of pond life and dappled shade, interrupted by a tree falling, and a sudden accident, which leads to a complex and violent climax. Image inversion is used early in the sequence, possibly indicating an early presentment of dissociation and disorientation. The 'hit' 'heat' sequence that ensues is associated with red, blood and percussive images and sounds, which are more obvious and immediate than the earlier, more diffuse, calmer images. The identity and reality of the characters, such as 'uncle', 'grandfather', and 'she', are more elusive and ambivalent. Most of the characters (with the possible exception of 'she') appear either hostile or unreliable. More than textual, verbal or

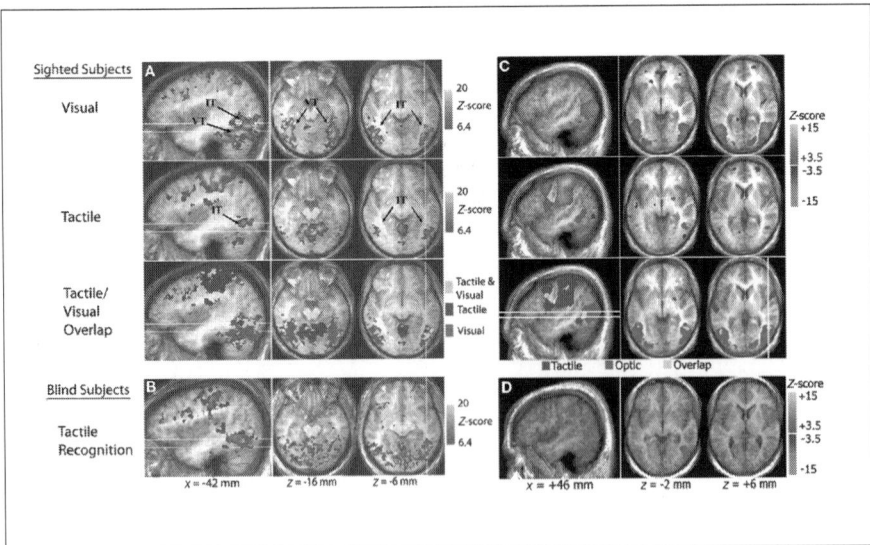

Neural response patterns in human brain, during visual and tactile recognition.
Inferior temporal (IT) and ventral temporal (VT) regions are indicated. The bottom sequence shows areas activated by both tactile and visual perception.
Reproduced with kind permission of Dr Kupers and Prof Pietrini from Kupers R, Pietrini P, Ricciardi E, Ptito M 2011, 'The nature of consciousness in the visually deprived brain', Frontiers, 2:19.doi:10.3389/fpsyg.2011.00019s

musical commentary, it is the visual images that appear closest to deeper experience and to artistic expression, in variety and depiction of mood and experience.

C o n c l u s i o n s : The sequence of images and commentary in IT, HEAT, HIT, while commenting on the reliability of perception and interpretation of reality, also suggest a perception of experience that may reflect the response of the viewer to images, ranging from the more direct and readily interpreted (heat, hit), to the more elusive and diffuse, the ambiguously defined 'it' in the title. It is suggested that the latter may be associated with the pleasurable images in the earlier sections of the narrative. It could be argued that the more complex imagery in this sequence is more closely associated with artistic expression.

PRIEST
Father Rob Wickham, Rector of Hackney

The opening sequence of words, asking me to focus and give this short film your undivided attention, is very effective. Following these in-structions, I was lulled into a false sense of security with the image of cooling waters that looked and felt so good.

The intensity of the music, images and countdown to the final minutes resembled scenes from the film *Ring*, which also included many images that bore no connection with each other on the surface.

I was being taken on a journey to places I recognised in Hackney, but also to the great unknown. I was left wondering who 'Uncle' was, I was left wondering who the five women talking about me were, I was left with the images of sharp knives, cut legs and breaking glass, all of which made me feel apprehensive, nervous and deeply unsettled.

SHOPKEEPER
Umit Seren

It's an unusual film, or documentary, and it shows lots of wild life and natural habitats of animals. Men hiking up mountains. It's a magnificent portrait.

PSYCHOANALYST
Bogdan Wolf

Artists have no need of psychoanalysis, so goes the prejudice, because they make no use of repression. Freud introduced repression as a mechanism that protects the subject from the trauma of the unspeakable real. So repression pertains specifically to the field of speech and language. When speaking, the subject appears to circumscribe the hole of the real, the crack in the body, the "one leg missing in the pile", as the film's narrator tells us. But to be precise, it is the signifier of this experience that remains repressed. There are experiences at the dawn of life which are unrepresentable because when they take place the language misses its target. Sexuality, satisfaction are also impossible experiences. Trauma is the language's failed encounter with the real.

In the experience of encountering a work of art, which should be distinguished from the subject's encounter with the repressed and unrepresentable signifier, it is the spectator who represses 'the real' of the encounter. The spectator wants not to know, and therefore wants not to see what he watches. This refusal is relative to the primary repression.

The laws of art, we could say with Freud, follow a different path, that of sublimation. In sublimation there is no repression. Can visual art be approached as a bridge between sublimation and repression? Can art succeed where the language fails? Or is the language of art subject to the same laws of the signifier. What is an image? It is a pure signifier. It stands alone, except that it in an associative sequence, connected to other signifiers by way of differentiation of form, shape, colour, size, sharpness. No two images are identical because no two signifiers are identical.

The film sequence unfolds, moving from one image to another, interlacing the image of the chopping of a carrot with the text "your leg branches out like a metal line going directly into your mouth", and the image of a boy jumping into the water with the sound of a shattering glass on impact. You must "eat the image", the narrator says. Eat your *Dasein*, Lacan says. Eat your existence, your language, live what you are made of, breath what you have been spoken to. But what is the sense of the boy jumping, the glass shattering, of the narrator suddenly gasping for air when an image of a dog and a text saying 'grabbed Mark's leg' appear?

The visual sequence is organised like an analytic session without an analyst. Interpretation remains unpunctuated and the unconscious is left to itself, to art. I will shatter glass into pieces in front of you and show you the soft feather, and the green frog spawning to life, and a naked woman holding a bunch of parsley, not over her pubic hair or breast, as we would stereotypically assumed, but over her belly, the mother's sacred place, and you tell me what I want.

The unconscious spits out the images, the narrator speaking all the time. It speaks about the granddad, the uncle who 'pushed the onlookers into the water', and the sizzling of the charcoal — 'it smells red' — red meat, a body, the uncle. Something went wrong, terribly wrong, and the scenes indicate this, giving us a warning. Something is always wrong, there are punches, smell of blood, and them, the women using sharp words, while the spectator witnesses a spiky, sharp ball and an apple with protruding pins and needles. There is a sound of a siren that strangely attracts us — like the ancient sirens Odysseus resisted — to the clingy sound of a car crash, shattered glass, again.

Tell me about my desire. What do I want in this? If the artist knows the truth of his or her desire it is in the sense of not saying it but showing it. Showing also means hiding, concealing, masking. But it is in the mask that we read what by concealing it at the same time reveals. The fantasy reveals what real satisfaction is at stake. The gaze is the axis of the visual encounter. Around it gyrate the spectator and the one looked at, and something else that slips away from this symmetry. The provocation of the gaze provokes sexual satisfaction. Being looked at is always enjoyed. It does not make sense, has no meaning yet, but is enjoyed, occluding, preventing, perhaps prolonging the refusal to know. The artist looks at the cars, frogs, feathers, cracked rocks, the sea, and they look back at her. In his youth, Lacan was once on a ship and the sailor asked him 'when you look at that can of sardines does it look at you?'

It is not by accident that Freud, who did not say much about the gaze, spoke of art as a representation of fantasy. The mother ('room full of men smoking like in your mother's room'), the granddad, the uncle, the women — we have a family scene where the father remains hidden, untouched, yet present in his absence. There are scenes of violence, punches, smashed glass, car crash and the determination of life spawned to continuation, as if wrapped up in the images, and lyrical moments of repose. The images support life, perhaps protect it. The unconscious, as a structure of language, remains at the back, knotting the paths of images that remain enigmatic, just as the mask remains enigmatic. At the end there is a lingering, meandering quantity of smoke. It is what remains.

GHOSTWRITER
Jane Gifford

Let go, and I'll catch you…
She let go.
He didn't. He didn't catch her. He laughed.
The taste of fear, the smell of disappointment, the sentence of missed opportunity. All in six minutes of snapshot staccato and searing solitude. We look on, we follow our instructions, we concentrate, we try, we try so very hard to comply and to trust what we are seeing and what we are told. Why do we trust? Why do we want to trust? Not simply want, we long to trust, to trust others we admire — with our emotions, our friendship, our need for love. But not uncle, whose sinister, creeping presence lurks without conscience — never trust 'uncle'.
The tree is sawn. The trunk topples. The words fall from the ceiling like a branch — with power and momentum — missing our feet, but not our stomachs that quail with the gut- twisting certainty of disaster that is so far beyond our control as mere spectators.
All these images, so perfectly and beautifully executed, with a precision and eye for stunning detail. Fingernail in walnut shell. Like dreams in Technicolor and stereophonic surround sound, building up the story of chase, and longed-for, long-promised escape.
Images and words. Words that are presented as images. White on black. Cling to them. They are the only safe forms. Again trust. I want more words in white because they tell me good things and they anchor my soul that is so badly in need of stability and relief from the horrid, screechy, angry, ugly images — just feed me more words.
Attempts at pacifying — with water and calm words — don't add up to anything more than further deceit. 'We will be nice to you now' is found to be a lie as aggressive as any amputation of leg or shattering of glass. We

live out our six minutes in the hope of better things to come — surely good things to come; surely kindness is only a waft away and we shall then relax and smile and clap and congratulate. But we are disappointed — we have jumped and not been caught and we suspect there is much hurtful, acidic laughter.

THE BUTCHER'S WIFE
S Mely

First I want to congratulate you for putting together a very interesting piece of film.

It was very interesting how you described your words and put them together with the clips. Your clips were very sharp and clear.

I wish you the best of luck for the future.

~~too~~ This was not an ordinary piece of clip.

I found it ~~very~~ very modern and different.

It was quick to understand but you really have to concentrate and watch very carefully.

Very different indeed.

Good Luck

S Mely

GRACE SCHWINDT
WITH MARINA VISHMIDT

FIVE
SCRIPTS

LOCATION 1

G: He talked about the most efficient ways of making use of time:
    of how to create multiple schedules and of how to go to bed with
    an empty inbox. This was something he was an expert on in his
    lifetime, but it of course acquired a metaphysical dimension.

M: But even if he really does enjoy it, that subjective happiness does
    remember ideology.

G: From the outside, the bourgeois concept of freedom left the
    way open for the recognition of metaphysical authorities,
    and this permits external unfreedom to be perpetuated within
    the human soul.

M: This influences the ruthless mode of individuation in terms
    of complete subjugation of the worker's self.

    [*Opens kitchen hatch.*]

G: One must abandon all attempts at self-definition.

M: What happens to a person within an art institution who does not
    have any more questions to ask?

G: The idea that freedom consists of self-determination is
    pathetic — but choices come from somewhere.

    [*The cupboard collapses under the weight of her touch.*]

M: Yet bourgeois philosophy put the autonomy of the person
    right at the centre of its theory. Freedom was assigned to the
    inner sphere of the person. At the same time, the outer person
    was subjected to the system of worldly powers. The system of
    autonomy and reason.

G: The concept of self-determination has nothing to do with
    freedom. Kant: autonomy means obeying yourself.

M: It is the fuel that allows common people to attain uncommon results.

G: Perhaps doing nothing has a potential of conditioning some kind of autonomy. But what does silence means to autonomy or resistance? Ie. a discourse takes place even when it's not verbalised.

M: One can become aware of his or her potential to exist and create only when this potential is not realised.

[*Advances and stretches out her hand.*]

G: Silence as resistance would have to distort the parameters of organised speech — the becoming-visible of a subject through speech, in order to escape its destiny of being a performative mode within that situation.

M: The real master over his work. The autonomously acting person and at the same time this person is sought in contradistinction to his lifeless works, as the negativity of work.

G: The moonlight was so bright it seemed like daytime.

[*Opens the window.*]

M: The individual can't be free and unfree, autonomous and heteronomous, unless the being of the person is conceived as divisible and belonging to various spheres.

G: The subjection could only be claimed, otherwise you are still performing, perhaps in an art educational context where anything can be individualised as a practice.

[*Feels the velvet upholstery against her leg.*]

M: Relapse into barbarism is always an option — a certain measure of freedom and, conversely, submission. A destiny at once dreamy and rational. Freud: death-drive.

G: Two essential elements of the mental attitude of he who is subject
to authority. A certain measure of freedom, the tying of will to
the authoritative will of order.

M: A great deal will be gained if we succeed, through therapy, in
transforming your historical mystery into everyday unhappiness.

[*Trips and falls.*]

G: It's this whole thing of subjection. The constitution of the subject
by the discipline of speech. Then entering into the symbolic
order and so forth.

M: The inner freedom of man, his pure will proved they remain
pure, can't be broken. It has failed, however, to eliminate the
need for a subject of some kind.

[*Holds her hair.*]

G: Freedom is not the freedom to accumulate, but the fact that
I have no need to accumulate.

M: Freedom and unfreedom, autonomy and heteronomy, are yoked
in the same concept and united in the single person. Freedom
is the condition of unfreedom.

G: But here we seek him who's not done as works are, but is an
initiator and a master of work.

[*Her movement traces a tight circle. She doesn't stop.*]

M: Human beings become their own property. The idea of freedom
from labour is replaced by choosing one's own work.

[*Lies flat on the floor and tries to fit through a small gap that leads
to fresh air.*]

G: Women should acquire the right to dispose of their own bodies.
That is threatened by sex.

M: Why should a woman give up her seat in the cattle car for a bloody struggle she could not hope to win?

G: Once again the limitations are so extreme.

M: I can't imagine it could present me with as stark an experience of alienation and loss.

[*Opens the door and speaks freely.*]

G: That only this strange mix of intuition and belief can be the right way to think, act and create. It almost becomes our methodology.

M: But though homosexuality is as limited and sick as our heterosexuality, a day may soon come in which our healthy trans-sexuality may be the norm.

[*Acts surprised, as if the story is incredible, despite knowing that it happened.*]

G: But if it proves to be even worse, that may be interesting.

M: You can either be governed willingly by stating your desires, or brutally.

G: But if you were to tell him about our idea that it is supposed to be enjoyable, he would rather that we left him in peace. Efficiency can be experienced as a form of terror.

[*Moves the armchair back to its original position.*]

M: But only because and in so far as man is free can he be unfree. The script I used is from the category entitled 'individual accounts'.

8 METAPHORS

LOCATION 2

M: The special tie women have with children is recognised by everyone. I submit, however, that the nature of this bond is no more than shared oppression.

G: Thus it was woman's reproductive biology that accounted for her original and continued oppression, and not some sudden patriarchal revolution.

M: The patriarchal family was only the most recent in a string of 'primary' social organisations. Childbearing capacity.

G: If we dismantle the family, subjection of so-called pleasure to reality, i.e. sexual repression, has lost its function.

M: But the 'revolution' had been won within a system organised around nuclear family. Within such a repressive structure, only a more sophisticated repression can result.

G: This thing — of women's alleged ability being used as alibi for the eventual degradation of working conditions for everyone — seems to come up in a lot of histories of labour movements. The joke is that after everyone was expected to work flexibly (as initially only women were supposed to since their main employment was unpaid and domestic), women still get sidelined for having families. That's how capitalism profits from gender ideology, while intensifying it into glaring contradictions and natural facts.

M: Turning to the past, while it offers no true model, is, however, of some value in understanding the relativity of oppression, though it has been a fundamental human condition. It has appeared to differing degree in different forms.

[*Sound of a lorry reversing outside can be heard.*]

G: But there's still an untried third alternative. You can attempt to develop a view based on sex itself.

M: The end of compartmentalisation of personality through reintegration of the sexual with the whole could have important cultural side effects.

G: Those women who persisted in demanding careers became, in turn, instruments of the repressive educational system. Their newfound insight, that babble of child psych social work, served to keep a fresh generation of women and children down.

[*Stranger can be heard outside. Stranger attempts to open the door. It is locked.*]

M: I recently read about changes in education at the turn of the century. And the claim was made that women were admitted to universities at a time when so-called 'analysis' and 'reason' were replaced by so-called 'expression' and 'understanding' in the humanities.

G: Reactionary schools of thought developed. Social science became 'functional', studying operations of institutions only within general value systems, thus promoting acceptance of status quo.

M: Psychology became reactionary to its core. Its potential as serious discipline undermined by its usefulness to power.

[*Looks at classified adverts of rooms for rent.*]

G: I wonder whether criticism and verbalism is an expected attribute of students to be functional and effective, emptied of meaning.

M: The way communion transpires in education. Silence is failure.

G: I suppose it's about what circumstances would have to apply for silence to become political.

[*Emerges from the back room.*]

M: The desperate current state of affairs fills me with hope.

G: How does art education fit into defined relationship between work, labour, profit and so on?

M: Labour signs freedom.

G: But the opposite of work is regarded as nothing more than consumption.

[*Tidies the DVDs on the shelves.*]

M: Doer and deed, person and work are torn asunder. The person never enters into the work. The true human subject.

G: Society's material production has, in many instances, been rationalised down to the last detail. But, as a whole, I remain irrational.

M: Under this mode of production, intellectual and material labour is subject to endless division.

G: The division of labour will only be ended by elimination of labour!

M: If the world were so planned that everything one does served the whole of society in a transparent manner, I would be happy to spend two hours a day working as a lift attendant.

G: There is a level of reality that stems directly from economics.

M: With the rise of immaterial work, human language and creativity have become primary sources of value.

G: That has happened in many different ways and can be clearly seen, for example, in constant re-questioning of continued work to produce new conditions to produce.

M: The artist is no longer understood as self-centred subjectivity. The process of artistic creation is more research-orientated.

[*Sits down on log bench.*]

G: Can we talk about the difference of collaboration as practical for its own sake?

M: The problem is that caesura springs from a remedial but naïve hope that there is always something that is more real than relation in which we participate.

G: When collaboration fails to inflict change within the public sphere, it's not part of *res publica*—it can produce unrestrained forms of oppression.

M: We say that collaboration, communication and connection belong to the most fetishised fields of the present day.

G: In contemporary society, working together cannot be conceived as separate from time management.

M: When I was preparing for the conference I realised our failure was not only because of lack of time.

G: And the other becomes value in cooperation.

M: All strategies are equally unproductive.

[*Appears violent.*]

G: Some over-systematic thinkers oscillate between loaded denunciations of capitalism and the bourgeoisie, and their oppressive institutions on the one hand, and admiration on the other. They make society into the 'object'. This must be closed to be complete.

M: The bourgeoisie fought its greatest battles under the banner of reason. But bourgeois society deprives reason of its realisation.

G: The incompleteness of any impersonal system is where the personal comes in.

M: The union of internal autonomy and external heteronomy has dominated bourgeois theory since the reformation.

G: These antagonisms appear in the most varied forms. They are rational yet fortuitous, necessary yet bad.

M: Bourgeois theory has taken great pains to justify this.

G: The non-bourgeois is supposed to preserve itself in love.

M: The class analysis is a beautiful piece of work.

G: The concept of authority leads to the concept of freedom.

M: Two relatively self-enclosed spheres are set up, and freedom and unfreedom divided in such a way that one sphere is wholly a realm of freedom and the other a realm of unfreedom.

G: The fact that the production of life cannot be rationally mastered by the society breaks through in the theological and philosophical reflection of its existence.

M: For the full freedom of man would denote his complete liberation from God.

G: Strictly speaking there is no liberation of man in history, or Christian doctrine has good reasons for viewing such a liberation as something negative and evil. Liberation from God and freedom to sin.

M: The inner freedom of man, his pure belief, cannot be broken.

G: The power of authority, whether it does right or wrong, cannot harm the soul.

M: His subordination is a free act, which he does not 'owe' them.

G: However, this anti-authoritarian tendency is only the complement of an order that is tied to the functioning of opaque relationships of authority.

M: The condition of an animal at the level of reflection—that is freedom.

[*People heard talking outside.*]

G: Freedom would mean reverting to the chaotic, the diffuse.

M: Freedom means not having to work.

LOCATION 3

G: What is time then? I know very well what time is if not asked
    about it, but if somebody asks me what time is and I want
    to explain, I become confused.

    [*Touches her bare arm.*]

M: We just look foolish if we try to give explanations that are too
    precise.

G: My idea of exhaustion also comes from a resistance to idea
    that groups can claim that they have reached an exhaustion of
    criticism, e.g. on a historical period which I think assumes the
    possibility of resolvedness and also of ownership and of authority
    over a period.

M: Collaboration places people into the present time. It's only
    through collaboration that people can become visible where they
    add to the flow of money.

    [*Walks forward so slowly that it is almost unnoticeable.*]

G: At once highly general, the language of maths set out to
    discriminate between all these spaces as precisely as possible.

M: As object rather than subject, space came to dominate by
    containing them, senses and all bodies. Not so many years ago,
    the word space had geometrical meaning.

G: Those kinds of spaces where time thickens somehow, is no longer
   a permeable medium to speech.

[*Her body feels heavy in the water.*]

M: At the same time, only when the potential is not being actualised,
   one is opened to one's being in time.

G: The problem is that such exploitation of human potential
   structured collaboration as a mode where collaboration equals
   actualisation. An obsession with present time. This obsessive use
   means that we've no time at all.

[*Grabs her hand and runs.*]

M: In the circumstances planning would offer the best prospect.

[*Avoids being in the same space with her.*]

G: Indeed, each new form of state introduces its own particular way
   of partitioning space, its own particular way of discourses about
   things and people in space.

M: There is probably much that can be said on the subject of chairs.

[*Touches the tiles.*]

G: Specialised forms of work keep their audience appraised of
   all sorts of equalised spaces. Work, play, transportation, public
   facilities—all are spoken of in spatial terms. Even illness and
   madness are supposed to have their own space.

M: It's time to come back to the question of time.

G: I shall return later to kinship between mental space and the one
   of the technocrats in offices.

[*Feels the steam in her throat.*]

M: She describes the obsession with time management as trying to look behind the mask of death. My own thoughts tend to move in the direction of saying good people are dying out.

LOCATION 4

M: One might go so far as to explain social space in terms of prohibition: a male child is separated from his mother because incest is forbidden, and the prohibition which separates the child from his body because language breaks down the unmediated unity of the body. In other words, the male child suffers symbolic castration and his own phallus is objectified.

G: Hence, the Mother, her sex and her blood, are relegated to the realm of the cursed and the sacred; sexual pleasure is fascinating and inaccessible.

M: People repress their own chaotic drives which might lead them away from work.

[*Points at the screen.*]

G: In order to persuade human beings to work you have to fob them off about work as a thing in itself.

M: A shaft of light falls from the telos onto labour. But people misinterpret the light. Instead, they take labour as the telos and see their personal work succeed as that purpose. That is the secret. If they did not do that, such a thing as solidarity would be possible.

G: Work is the clue to making sure that all will be well. But by elevating it to god status, it is emptied.

M: On the one hand, Marx imagined liberation from work. On the other, social labour is seen in a very bright light.

G: No ideology survives in the camps. Whereas our society still
    insists that work is good.

    [*Takes the stairs and walks centre stage.*]

M: The uselessness of the work deprives people of the last bit
    of pleasure they might obtain from it.

G: I do not believe that human beings enjoy work.

M: Happiness is connected to work.

G: The worst thing is to mix up work and happiness. Shaft of light
    must be reflected back by resistance.

M: Do we only find happiness in our work because we are bourgeois?

G: Happiness would be an animal condition from perspective
    of whatever is animal.

M: Animals can teach us what happiness is.

G: Relapse into barbarism is always an option.

M: The only thing that goes against my pessimism is that fact that
    we still think. All hope lies in thought.

    [*Unheard.*]

G: Good people are dying out. In the circumstances, planning
    would offer the best prospect.

M: I would say that it's our duty to marry thinking with right
    practice.

G: There is something deluded about the separation of theory and
    practice. Separation is ideology.

M: Marx would have classed television and the motorbike
    as ideology.

G: It's not as if we should do something other than thinking. But rather that we should think differently and act differently.

[*Walks up on to the balcony and balances on the railing.*]

M: It really does call for great effort.

G: So does riding a motorbike.

M: That is a measurable effort. His true pleasure in motorbike riding is in the anal sounds it emits.

G: All that is delusion.

[*Stands behind the curtain.*]

M: Let us return to our invention of what the body has to give.

G: I have been thinking about physicality and mentality of the subject. It's perhaps necessary to resist this demand of efficiency in the context of capital production.

M: Firstly, the problem is that people are not regarded as profit but as cost. For example, I read that lower wages for women in Germany were justified by law through the assumed lesser physical strength of women. As a result, a lower efficiency.

[*Lies flat on the floor.*]

G: Moreover, the process is intensified through speeded-up power of invention not only nourish capital but constitute value. The most profitable investment.

M: I am also thinking about how, in certain professions, the individual is encouraged to find the most efficient ways of making use of time, to create manageable plans etc., and of how to go to bed with an empty inbox.

G: This acquires a metaphysical dimension. Time management as a desperate attempt to look behind the unbearable mask of death.

M: This relates very much to my idea of exhaustion in my work.

[*Sits down on seven different chairs in the auditorium.*]

G: A sense of exhaustion is also expressed in your work through movement. A double aspect: both using movement as the insertion of some language and a way to get out of language.

M: I'm also thinking about what role silence plays in this relationship between movement and language.

G: I understand the silence in your work as disruptive, the same as 'wrong' movements.

LOCATION 5

M: My idea of 'extra' also comes from a resistance to the idea that a group or a generation can claim that they have reached an exhaustion of criticism, for example, on a historical period which assumes the possibility of resolvedness, and also ownership, authorship over a period.

[*Walks between the chairs, counting them. Every time she reaches a hundred, she starts again at number one.*]

G: I see the current leftist analysis as outdated and superficial because this analysis does not relate to the structure of the economic class system to its origins in the sexual class system, the model for all other exploitative systems and thus the tapeworm that must be eliminated first by any true revolution.

M: Animals can teach us what happiness is.

G: Children are represented at every waking minute. Childhood is hell.

[*Looks to her left.*]

M: Might they be regarded as prefigurations of what would be less
   uncommon in a post-bourgeois world?

G: Teddy wants to rescue a pair of concepts: theory and practice.
   These concepts are themselves obsolete.

   [*Stands on top of a table.*]

M: But the rebellion was destroyed before they could eliminate these
   myths. They went underground and reappeared complicated by
   mass consumerism.

   [*Sits next to her on the stage, facing the empty space.*]

G: The worst thing is to mix up work and happiness.

M: What we ought to be protesting, rather than that children are
   being exploited like adults, is that adults can also be exploited.
   We want to be talking not about sparing children for a few
   years from the horrors of adult life, but about eliminating those
   horrors.

   [*Collects dust.*]

G: Happiness is connected to work.

M: Humanity has begun to outgrow nature and we can no longer
   have a discriminatory sex-class system on the grounds of its
   origin in nature.

G: Happiness would be an animal condition viewed from the
   perspective of whatever has ceased to be animal.

   [*Balances on a fallen column which connects the stage with the floor.*]

M: Feminists have to question not just all of Western culture,
   but the organisation of culture itself. Even the very organisation
   of nature.

[*Lies down next to the blackboard.*]

G: Whatever it is that allows subjects to identify social systems as
    open to change or to invest in it affectively, to identify with sets
    of rules that are seen as necessary but incomplete.

[*Lifts her right foot.*]

M: For the free Christian knows that he is raised above worldly law.
    and that his subordination to the worldly authorities is 'free' act,
    which he does not 'owe' them.

G: Our final step must be the elimination of the very conditions
    of femininity and childhood themselves that are now conducive
    to this alliance of the oppressed, clearing the way for a fully
    human condition.

[*Turns away from the stage.*]

M: The idea that freedom consists in self-determination is really
    rather pathetic.

                                    END

With adaptations from the following texts:

— Theodor Adorno and Max Horkheimer, 'Towards a new manifesto', 1956, *New Left Review,* no. 65, Sept–Oct 2010
— Herbert Marcuse, *A Study on Authority,* 1936, trans. Joris De Bres, London: Verso, 2008
— Bojana Kunst, 'Prognosis on Collaboration', *TkH Journal,* no. 17, October 2010
— Henri Lefebvre, *The Production of Space,* 1974, trans. Donald Nicholson-Smith, London: Blackwell, 1991
— Shulamith Firestone, *The Dialectic of Sex: The Case for Feminist Revolution,* 1970, New York: Bantam Books, 1979
— Personal correspondence between Grace Schwindt and Marina Vishmidt

SAMUEL STEVENS WITH
URIEL ORLOW AND MAIJA TIMONEN

DIFFICULTIES
IN WRITING THE TRUTH

SELECTED FILM STILLS
Uriel Orlow and Samuel Stevens

[A basement room, white walls, door open in background. A woman in her fifties or sixties sits at a table in the foreground, gesticulating with both hands as she speaks. She is wearing a green suit jacket and blouse. In front of her: a cup of tea, a white porcelain dish with sugar and a plate. Behind her: a classroom-sized writing pad, a shelf unit with books and a kettle on the floor.]

ESPERI, 10 m 14 s, DVCAM, 2005
Image location: Esperanto Society Headquarters, Bialystok, Poland, 2005
Image timecode 00:02:03:16

[Two Vietnamese men in winter coats and hats sitting on folding chairs over a cardboard box. They are playing a board game. A third man in jeans and baseball cap stands over them to the left, watching the game. Light falls into the scene from behind the third man. In the background: piles of plastic-wrapped garments, hanging coats and rows of shirts and tops. A street market.]

JARMARK EUROPA, 12 m 39 s, DVCAM, 2005
Image location: Jarmark Europa, Warsaw, Poland, 2005
Image timecode 00:02:16:06

[The criss-cross of a wire fence. Close behind the fence, looking into the camera: a bison with brown hair and curved horns. It stands at the edge of a fenced grassy compound. In the far distance: the faint outlines of wintry trees. A forest.]

ZUBR, 14 m 17 s, 16 mm / DV, 2006–10
Image location: Belavezhskaya Pushcha Zoo, Kamieniuki, Belarus, 2005
Image timecode 00:09:37:09

[A couple in their fifties or sixties stand at the far
end of a large circular platform enclosed by a low
wall. The couple are wearing holiday clothing;
sunglasses, short sleeves, sandals. Behind, a seascape:
a suspension bridge crosses the sea to the centre
of the horizon. The floor of the platform is tiled.
To the left the floor is painted with a map of North
Africa and Southern Europe joined by the bridge;
to the right is a large compass, the points are
marked with the letters: N, E, S, O.]

ATLANTROPA, 19 m 15 s, HD, 2009
Image location: Viewpoint on Ctrad e San Antonio, Ceuta, 2008
Image timecode 00:07:26:17

[People wearing winter coats and sunglasses and
carrying shopping bags walk along a street towards
us. The street is enclosed by stone walls on either
side. The wall on the left is in bright sunlight; the
wall on the right is obscured by an extreme shadow
that emerges behind and leads to a small plaza
enclosed by buildings. A subtitle reads 'people'.]

SIN PAPELES, 10 m 51 s, 16 mm / DV, 2005
Image location: Carrer d'Aroles, Barcelona, Spain, 2005
Image timecode: 00:01:57:00

THE DISTANT BEAST: PART 1
Maija Timonen

At first glance, Samuel Stevens' three films *Zubr, Jarmark Europa* and *Esperi* have two things in common: firstly, they all deal with language and, secondly, they were shot on a trip to Poland. *Zubr* depicts a nature reserve that falls on the border between Poland and Belarussia. It ties together information and personal stories about reserve by using the 'zubr' (the name for wisent or bison in many east European languages) as a guiding figure. *Jarmark Europa* shows Vietnamese stallholders at one of the largest outdoor markets in Europe, situated in Warsaw. *Esperi* is filmed at an Esperanto club in Bialystok.

On closer consideration, it is apparent that these films foreground language as their subject matter in order to use it as a pathway to decipher complex social formations. The fact that all three films are primarily shot in one country (parts of *Zubr* are also filmed in Belarus) encourages thoughts not only about that specific location, but also about its 'country-ness' and about where the idea of a nation lies in contemporary Europe. Stevens' films comprise a subtle aesthetic of belonging, and verbal language is simply one channel for reflections on inclusion or lack thereof. As an artist travelling to a foreign country, his position within these social determinations becomes inevitably central to the films.

In *Zubr*, two types of text are presented: subtitles and text screens recount a story, but each adopt a different register. The subtitles narrate in the first person, while the text screens convey background historical research. A discrepancy between these two modes (the former, a subjective viewpoint; the latter, the construction of objectivity) is a consistent feature, and both are engaged in a deceptive struggle for domination. One seems to be working from a position of mute disadvantage: the subtitles act as the narrator's 'voice' but are not accompanied by audible speech, and are therefore not backed up by the material / sensory dimension that would lend the subjective voice validity against officially accepted truths. Reminiscent of subtitles in a foreign language film, this 'translation' is without the 'original' that should go with it—that is to say, the original spoken language that any subtitles merely interpret.

Benedict Anderson refers to nation states as imagined communities, whose inception and imagery were tied to the rise of vernacular languages facilitated by advancements in printing technologies.[1] Nineteenth-century European nationalist imaginary was constructed around rendering in writing what previously only existed in speech. The constructed primacy of the written over the spoken that followed the inception of industrial-scale printing has also trickled down to the voiceless subtitles of *Zubr*. Writing takes over and the missing 'original language' seems to ever so subtly pose questions about the formalised guises of national identity.

Although appearing to counter the 'text screens' of historical facts, there is something officially sanctioned about the subtitles too. The relationship between the subjective viewpoint represented by them, and the assumed historical objectivity represented by the text screens, is more complex than merely one of opposing positions. Rather, they join in alluding to the constructed nature of an 'official line', and perhaps of nationality as one manifestation of it.

With their missing material reference point of speech, the subtitles also formally resemble Anderson's description of nationalist imagery as having the character of a replica without an original.[2] He conjures this idea through discussing national monuments and the contentless seriality they exemplify. The Tomb of the Unknown Soldier is one example of a transferable and reproducible form that points to a material origin missing in action. This type of monument can be found in countries around the world. It pertains to speak to the experience of war specific to whichever country in which it is situated, despite its ubiquitous generality. It follows this same formal logic in the way it puts forward the singularity of the soldier as meaningful, though nothing is known of him, he has no identity and he could belong anywhere. There is something of the figure of the zubr, and the film's exploration of the multiple objects it provides a name and an image for, that is reminiscent of such seriality. As an emblem of strength and resilience in true national way, 'zubr' is the name of a Polish brand of

1   Benedict Anderson, *Imagined Communities: Reflections of the Origin and Spread of Nationalism*, London: Verso, 1991.

2   Benedict Anderson, 'Replica, Aura and Late Nationalist Imaginings', *The Spectre of Comparisons: Nationalism, Southeast Asia and the World*, London: Verso, 1998, pp. 48.

beer. But the term, like the forest in which the animal 'zubr' is found (and the animal itself) transcends borders: it was also the name of a Belarussian youth opposition group that dissolved its own finite form, eventually giving up its name in order to join forces with the broader opposition struggle in the country.

The stories recounted by the voiceless person who narrates the subtitles, further evoke the shifts and internal contradictions of nationality as a form of belonging, using language as a key into these. Panning away from the specificities of the films location on the border of Poland and Belarussia, the narrator describes an encounter with a Basque man on a train in Spain, who refers to Euskara as 'his' language and who then, when quizzed on the matter, confesses to being unable to speak the language.

If *Zubr* raises thoughts about national identity as an artefact—in the literal sense of a manmade object—then Esperi folds this very question of human product back into language. Stevens interviews the chairwoman at the Esperanto Society Headquarters (located in the hometown of Ludwig Lazarus Zamenhof, its inventor). She attempts to explain the ideals of universal communication behind the language, speaking in Esperanto without subtitles as if to illustrate how easily it can be understood. Aside from the sense of something constantly slipping through the gaps of comprehension, the viewer is presented with the mounting feeling that the speaker is constrained by the language she is speaking, indeed perhaps because of its simplicity. And a break does occur: the speaker meets the limits of the ideal of internationalism and is forced to revert back to her native Polish. This might also provide an allegory for the persistence or even a now historical resurgence of the nation as a form of political organisation, as indicated by the 'new' nation states formed in the wake of the fall on the Soviet Union.[3]

The setting of *Esperi* encapsulates the contradictions inherent to all forms of collectivity expressed as a 'belonging-to': it happens at the premises of what could be thought of as club for a universal language. In *Jarmark Europa*, the filmmaker becomes the one excluded from the 'club'—the social grouping that both stems from and informs a sense

---

3   This question is present in *Zubr* too, where there exists a tension (though not a contradiction) between unified Europe with Poland as its representative, and Belarussia as a post-soviet nation state.

of identity. Vietnamese market traders in Warsaw are filmed as they go about their business and chat to each other. English subtitles appear, but the person behind the video camera does not know what the people in front of it are saying. The presence of the camera creates an obvious divide between the observer and the observed, but the power dynamics that the technological barrier would normally signify, are flipped. A situation that could easily be read as the privileged European artist resting his objectifying gaze on the exotic other, is transformed as he becomes the butt of jokes.

Playfully disparaging comments emanate from the mouths of the documented subjects who appear to use their shared language as a shield. The travelling artist is simultaneously expelled and spoken into the picture. On screen, images also follow the air of indecision regarding the role of the artist as observer: they are sparse and stylistically representative of a certain aesthetic of artist documentary. And though this adherence to a specific 'style' communicates that they are a product of a self-conscious and deliberate aesthetic approach, the image also seems to serve the purpose of writing the author out, of muffling the authorial voice.

The three films are about borders. The market traders of *Jarmark Europa* are immigrants who, having crossed borders, demarcate the boundaries of their community that has been constructed within another. In *Esperi*, it is the dream of transcending borders and language barriers (and the persistence or dissolution of this dream) that provides the subject matter. In *Zubr*, it is revealed that the border between Poland and Belarussia, where the film was shot, is known as the 'lace curtain' (a play on 'the iron curtain' that previously existed in its place). This boundary separating EU from the east is full of holes. Policing the perforated line and the difficulty that this endeavour presents, again introduces the reflexive artist. One of the stories told in *Zubr* is recounted by the forest ranger: an artist was given permission to film in the protected primeval part of the forest on the condition he would act as a border guard, reporting any illegal immigrant he sees in the forest attempting to cross over from Belarussia to Poland. The position of visual power that the artist assumes (and subsequently the power over his subjects that the artist possesses) resonates with this story. This works both in relation to the general noun 'the artist', and to the specific artist Samuel Stevens who makes the video.

Most of *Zubr* is shot on 16mm film. This choice of medium is aesthetically specific and has the effect of ossifying its subjects and the surrounding terrain. Although approached in a documentary vein, the images seem trapped within the boundaries of some past or present no-time of the flickering film and its grainy beauty. It would be easy to critique medium specificity as fetishistic or exemplary of a non-specific nostalgia for a certain 'look'. But its use in *Zubr* is more meaningful. It confines the landscape and people depicted behind the screen of obsolescence, thus making material the barriers being recounted—social, geographical and political. Such materiality carries over to the films epilogue, shot this time with a handheld video camera. The scene shows a wisent in the forest, caught by the camera through coincidence and good fortune. This concluding digital image gives a glimpse of the materiality of the 'original' that persistently eludes capture throughout most of the film. The film in its entirety, a manmade artefact, finds its 'origin' in the digital artefact and the unintended distortions introduced by available technology. The pixelated face-off with the distant wisent, coupled with the heavy breathing of the cameraman, briefly return the film to the wild and to a more direct relation between the artist and his subject.

THE DISTANT BEAST: PART 2
Maija Timonen

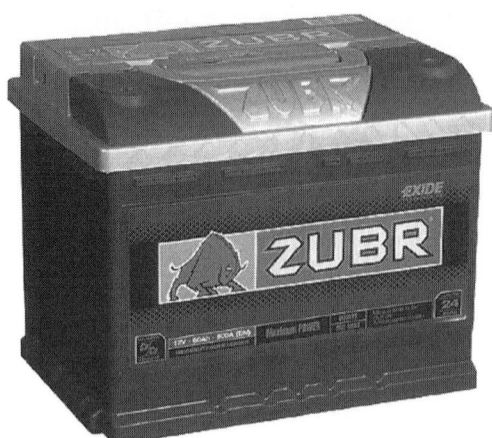

CORRESPONDENCE
Uriel Orlow and Samuel Stevens

7 January 2011

Dear Sam,
I hope you've had a good and relaxing break in the country. I, for
my part, enjoyed London stilling and slowing over the holidays—
and also watching your films again.
One of the things that struck me as I watched your films in
chronological order was the marked shift in documentary modality
between Atlantropa and the previous works. The trio of films made
in Belarus and Poland, ESPERI, JARMARK EUROPA *and* ZUBR, *as*
well as SIN PAPELES, *subscribe to an engaged, realist documentary*
methodology. Yet the truth quotient of ATLANTROPA *is of a different*
order. You describe the film as "set in an imagined present, centred
around a bridge spanning the Straits of Gibraltar". The bridge
doesn't exist but this does not mean it has no claim on reality.
In your carefully calibrated publication WHEN I SIT DOWN TO
WRITE, *I read about the very real (but never realised) 1920s project*
by German architect Hermann Sörgel to dam the Straits of Gibraltar
and thus link Europe and Africa. You also include an extract of
Arthur C Clarke's 1979 novel THE FOUNTAINS OF PARADISE,
which contains the first mention of an actual bridge across the straits
of Gibraltar. I hesitate to introduce the notion of 'fiction' here, as
I don't find the opposition of fact / fiction it presupposes very useful,
but if a term is needed, then something like 'possible facts' or
'probable reality' both seem to point towards a troubling of facticity
without getting stuck in the rigid binary opposition of fact and fiction.
So, thinking about the politics of facticity and the constructions of
the world you present, the distinction between the earlier films and
ATLANTROPA *is, perhaps, not that marked after all.*
This brings me to a first (somewhat long-winded) question: all your
films make reference to (and indeed originate in an engagement with)
historico-political events or social realities. You write that ATLANTROPA
"re-contextualises a BBC news article" from 2005 that reported the

*deaths of at least five people during a mass attempt by migrants to
get into the Spanish enclave of Ceuta, North Africa. How does this
re-contextualisation work and what is at stake for you in the
re-contextualising of this material? And more generally, what role
does specificity play in your films?*

*While there is a red thread going through your films, namely
that of a common concern or question mark around the politics and
representation of migration — be it in the Esperanto project, the
Vietnamese community in a street market in Poland, the
re-introduction of the Bison in Belarus, or the hunger-strike by
migrant workers without papers in Spain in 2001 — the films avoid
generalisation and instead always remain close to the specific context
at hand. So what I mean by 'specificity' is a kind of faithfulness
to particulars, which seems to be connected to notions of ethics and
responsibility (towards subjects). Sorry, it's a bit of a big question
to launch into, but it's something that I'm thinking a lot about
in my own work.*

Uriel

13 January 2011

Dear Uriel,
*Your question regarding how the re-contextualisation of the BBC
news report works is difficult to answer; the effects of re-telling this
story are complex to measure in an audience, and even more difficult
to pre-empt in the construction of the work at the editing stage.
So whether it does 'work' or not I cannot tell. For this reason, the
departure from a 'realist documentary methodology' was a gamble
(and it was also a steep learning curve for me at that time), but one
I undertook because I felt that the realist documentary form and news
report formats are too much of a platitude.*
*Cultivating a new method really emerged from an anxiety over the
effect of conventional or accepted forms within news media,
documentary and fine art. I wanted to create something that compelled
the audience to question these forms of representation, to somehow
command the viewer to independently consider the situation that the*

story described through its delivery. Works such as Isidore Isou's
TREATISE ON SLOBBER AND ETERNITY *and Peter Handke's*
OFFENDING THE AUDIENCE *influenced me in this respect. Although*
both of these works initial address is the form in which they are
written, I felt that they affronted their audience in the act of looking,
and I wanted to present the news report with this same mechanism.
So what was at stake, initially at least, was the affect in the viewer,
of the work.

This prioritisation risked faithfulness to particulars, or perhaps the
moral 'responsibility' that you describe, through distortion. It broke
a consensus agreement of an ethically correct documentary method.
In the earlier films, the narrator or the subject is always at the centre
of the film, and the voice indicates a faithfulness to particulars in the
moral sense. In the case of SIN PAPELES *and* ZUBR, *it is myself;*
in ESPERI, *it is the president of the Esperanto Society; with*
JARMARK EUROPA, *it's the market traders. This is an ethical*
condition that perhaps stems from the problem of 'speaking for
others'. You could say that ATLANTROPA *is more general in its lack*
of a central subject—it violates this condition with a voice-of-god
perspective.

The opening and closing shots of ATLANTROPA *directly address this*
condition of moral responsibility by breaking it, the subject is
documented but the circumstance disallows both a voice or control
over their image. JARMARK EUROPA *starts in this same direction,*
and although the work attempts to redeem its position of
responsibility through the provision of subtitles, it remains
uncomfortable. The decision to include these very invasive shots of
people at the border
at the beginning and end of ATLANTROPA *was difficult (as was*
shooting them). As can be read from their reaction to being filmed
(in the first shot the young men give the viewer the finger and in the
last shot the woman hides her face from view), there is an attempt
to redeem control of their own image from this intrusion, as a
universal ethical condition has been broken. I felt that this 'ethical
condition' needed to be complicated and passed on to the viewer
as he or she is also complicit in this act.

The 'correct' methodology felt too conventional; its association with
realism was illusory. The anxiety I described was that, in general,

a viewer's response to indicators of documentary realism may be too reflexive; the form has become ethically reassuring to them, thus diminishing the need for individual ethical judgement. News media relies on a similar confidence in its own 'ethical code' — to remove its rhetorical bias from the judgement of the individual. Of course, we are conscious of this when digesting news, but it is surprising how effective news media remains in shaping opinion in a general sense. What is ultimately at stake for me is that real situations are not excluded from cultural discourse and memory, and that sanctioned forms of representation are questioned. In the same way that I have constructed a possible reality by visualising a bridge across the Gibraltar Straits, the EU authorities control perception of the world by restricting images of the border fences. Despite status as fact or fiction, both actions relate to a particular part of the collective and individual imagination or conscience. I am trying to address the construction and our perception of the world by asking the viewer to consider the world consciously. I think that should be the basis of any moral judgement.

Sam

21 January 2011

Dear Sam,
It's interesting that you bring up Isou's TREATISE ON SLOBBER AND ETERNITY *and Handke's* OFFENDING THE AUDIENCE; *both of these directly address and thus implicate the audience, creating a kind of ethical bond.*
At the beginning of SIN PAPELES *you also quote Orwell: "When I sit down to write a book, I do not say to myself, 'I am going to produce a work of art'. I write it because there is some lie I want to expose, some fact to which I want to draw attention, and my initial concern is to get a hearing". It is this urgency to expose something that is at the heart of the 'ethics of faithfulness', and which I see in your work. I agree that conventional documentary realism no longer produces this condition because it often remains in a consensual comfort zone.*

*Your work creates an intriguing complication between image, sound
and language. In* SIN PAPELES, *the image is silent and the textual
inter-titles are accompanied by location sound, while* ZUBR *uses
overlayed text on the image. In* JARMARK EUROPA *there is a tension
between the incomprehensible conversation of the Vietnamese market
traders and the post-hoc translation in the subtitles.* ATLANTROPA,
*on the other hand, is accompanied by a deep, authoritative male
voice-over, whose account of Andalusia and the bridge across the
Straits of Gibraltar mixes fact and fiction and is, in turn, accompanied by Brahms' sweeping Fourth Symphony — music that was
used in the soundtrack to Luis Buñuel's* LAS HURDES *(1933), whose
fictional documentary mode serves as a precedent. In* Esperi, *you
defer the act of speaking entirely to your Esperanto interviewee.
So, interestingly, in each of the films you experiment with and
indeed propose a different usage of language in relation to the image.
The act of speaking, of addressing the audience, is always a
self-conscious one, not just on your part but also on the part of the
viewer. We become aware of the linguistic constructions, conventions
and aberrations. In his famous, posthumously published book,*
HOW TO DO THINGS WITH WORDS, *JL Austin analysed speech acts
on three levels: the performance of an utterance, the semantic force
of the utterance, and its actual effect. Your selective use of the
different modes of enunciation (intertitles, subtitles, voice-over) makes
me acutely aware of these levels. I would be interested to know a bit
more about your choice of narrative system in the respective films.
But returning to the notion of specificity, it seems to be me that there
is a dialectic at play in your work which we haven't yet touched on.
Each film makes reference to a specific historical and political moment,
context or project. All of these could be grouped together under the
generic (i.e. non-specific) notion of migration. What is played
out between your general interest in and commitment to questions of
migration and the specific moments or episodes you chose to focus on?*

Uriel

31 January 2011

Dear Uriel,

JL Austin's questioning of truth values and his findings allow us to step away from the polarity of true / false (which, like fact / fiction, I agree is unhelpful) and consider the performative aspect of communication outside of theatrical association. This is interesting in considering documentary film, political and journalistic rhetoric.
The films' different narrative systems were the result of the modes in which they were produced. ATLANTROPA *was very much preconceived as landscape shots with a narrative voice over that related to Buñuel's* LAS HURDES *and further back to travel or slide lectures performed at the beginning of the last century. The structure of* JARMARK EUROPA *and* ESPERI *both came very much out of the location situation and both narratives were shaped primarily in the editing process, whereas the narratives in* SIN PAPELES *and* ZUBR *were created in post-production through research and writing. Although the methods are different, I feel that the intention of these works are very much the same. Ultimately, I wished to avoid declaring or suggesting fixed ideas of truth and being didactic, by presenting an unstable yet coherent narrative system in each case.*
Orwell's quote expresses an urgency to expose, as you previously identified, a 'faithfulness to ethics'. It was this prioritisation over artistic concerns, rather than a claim to establish a notion of fact over fiction, or indeed truth over a lie that most inspired me. The influence of and reference to LAS HURDES *in* ATLANTROPA *is similar, Buñuel's urgency to expose the situation is documented as his priority over an attempt to profess a 'truthful' representation or declare a truth. Bertolt Brecht was also working in the inter-war period with a similar desire to expose the condition of the present, and this is strongly felt in his political writings, such as the introduction to his short essay* FIVE DIFFICULTIES IN WRITING THE TRUTH, *which begins: "Today anyone who wants to fight lies and ignorance and to write the truth has to overcome at least five difficulties. He must have the courage to write the truth, even though it is suppressed everywhere; the cleverness to recognise it, even though it is disguised everywhere; the skill to make it fit for use as a weapon; the judgement to select those in whose hands it will become effective;*

the cunning to spread it amongst them".
Brecht's notion of truth also presents us with a condition of
oppositional extremes in this statement, as does Orwell's presentation
of fact and lies in the preceding quote. Both are indicative of the
political rhetoric of the time, which although relating to a different
political situation nonetheless has an ethical insistence and
commitment to their political perspective with which I can identify
and which I believe is still relevant to cultural production today. This
may explain the feeling you had of an underlying political perspective
that you characterised as a 'red' theme running through my work.
This informs the selection of specific subjects in my own work and
constitutes a general concern. I also see this as an extension or
extra-narrative construction throughout the body of my work.
Migration is interesting to me because, as Alain Badiou identifies
in an interview with Peter Hallward, "the category 'immigrant' has
been systematically substituted for the category 'worker', only to
be supplanted in its turn by the category of the 'clandestine' or illegal
alien" in order to remove the reference to the worker from the
political discussion. This misrepresentation withdraws rights that
should be entitled to anyone working within the greater economy
of capitalism, and the inequality in the economic system points to
peoples' reasons for wanting to leave their place of origin. It is this
redefinition of the present condition, for political and economic ends,
that compels me to address the subject of migration rather than
phenomena of migration itself. Other specific subjects in my work
include the suppression of the Belarusian language in ZUBR, *the*
imperialistic dominance of the English language touched on in
ESPERI, *and the nationalistic construction of landscape imagery in*
FALLING LEAVES; *so the theme of migration should be seen as one*
specific part of this greater general concern.
Therefore, what is played out between my general interest and
commitment to specific moments is an attempt to express my political
perspective and idea of truth about the present situation without
insisting on a choice between oppositional extremes. I am attempting
to associate the ethical conditions of considering a subject (and indeed
the act of representation) with the politics of the present situation in
order to implicate the viewer. My reason for doing so is I feel that art
as a shared or public form of expression should be understood as

a political act, as I believe all collaborative determinations in life are. I also feel I need to acknowledge and appeal to acknowledgement of complicity in the present situation as to remain silent is to agree with it as it stands.

Sam

Sam,
Finally, we should also consider the image itself. The shots in your films are carefully framed: the camera lingers on evocative forest scenes in ZUBR *and breath-taking vistas in* ATLANTROPA; *the frame sets up haptic relationships between buildings and people in* ESPERI, JARMARK EUROPA *and* SIN PAPELES. *In each case, it seems that aesthetics, or even beauty plays an integral role.*

Uriel

Uriel,
In all of the films I have attempted to utilise the aesthetic as part of both the concept and delivery of the narrative, rather than generally subscribe to or avoid an aesthetic altogether. The materialistic feel of 16 mm film SIN PAPELES *is important to the practical separation of sound and image with that medium, while* ZUBR *uses both film and video which relates to its consideration of artifice and nature. Film is an interesting medium because it is so immersive.*
The aesthetic of the image plays an important function in drawing the viewer in and throwing them out of the work. By showing an aesthetically immersive or even conventionally beautiful image, I seek to throw the stability of that convention into question, just as in the case of the lingering shot of the forest that gives way to the interior sound of a ticket hall. The picturesque landscape in ATLANTROPA *has an aesthetic quality similar to postcard or tourist imagery, yet*

*it gives way to elements within the landscape that are contradictory
to what that aesthetic represents to the viewer. I try to work this idea
of beauty with and against the viewer's expectations, to present
the viewer with something that they think they feel comfortable in
understanding, and ask them to reconsider.*

Sam

STINA WIRFELT WITH
ANONYMOUS, DOMINIC PATERSON AND
DEBORAH STRATMAN

CUTTING ABOUT

THE JOKER

A Game of Incidental Urban Poker

—

Workshop for a Non-Linear Architecture

Amongst the various found objects which the *dérive* bestows upon its protagonists, the renegade playing card is a common yet always unexpected gift. The most potent examples usually fall into one of two distinct categories. On the one hand there are those cards whose decayed composition displays a wealth of surface patterning and texture. Such cards, by the nature of their reversion, are frequently so inscribed as to merit inclusion amongst those other found texts or graphic ensembles that illustrate the pages of *The Book of Psychogeography*. Experience has shown that these cards are rare, and to date your author has only come across two such examples during a four-year period of conscious *dérive*.

A much more frequent occurrence however – which both practical experimentation and the laws of probability suggest should account for approximately one half of all cards discovered – is that of the playing card found face down. Such situations are almost always accompanied by an immediate sense of exaggerated anticipation – *which of the fifty-five possibilities have been encountered?* The response can vary, from an immediate desire to turn the card over to a masochistically prolonged pleasure in attempting to envision (in a manner similar to the techniques utilised in co-ordinate visualisation exercises) what might possibly exist on the other side.

In the spring of 1994, during a prolonged series of *dérives* constructed as a consequence of the WNLA instigated *Driftnet* project, a coincidentally large number of such playing cards was discovered. Beginning on a particularly hot and humid April afternoon in the lanes running parallel to the north of the Sauchiehall Street pedestrianised zone (a negative psychogeographic *sink* long since avoided by the navigators of the Glasgow section), a card was discovered lying face down in the dirt beside the stage door of the Theatre Royal. It possessed no particular psychogeographical characteristics at the time of its discovery, primarily because of the exigencies of the constructed *dérive* then being undertaken. The card, a stained and faded three of diamonds, was however incorporated into the documentary findings pertinent to the *dérive*.

The chance encounter of a playing card occurs on average about one in every ten to fifteen *dérives*. (The figure must remain as imprecise as this since no formal statistical analysis has been conducted – the number has been derived purely from anecdotal and remembered experience.) The discovery the next day of another card, again found face down, came therefore as something of a surprise. The card, outside the front door of the Griffinette – the side bar adjacent to the Griffin Pub on King Street – was immediately seized upon and, with a distinct sense of *déjà vu*, cautiously turned over. Its revelation as the four of diamonds immediately shocked the attention of the individual in question, invigorating his imagination with a heightened reverie whose reverberations collided between the nature of such coincidence and the possibilities of discovering a five.

It had long been acknowledged amongst the fluctuating body of WNLA drift participants that encounters with coincidence were one of the more potent, if least understood, reasons for the empowerment of any given *dérive*. An analytical examination of how coincidence operated upon the navigational patterns of the dériving individual had often been suggested, but no one had ever been able to draft even the slightest of coherent texts. The general consensus that finally developed was that those specific coincidences to have played an important role in any given moment or situation of note should be alluded to for the time being only through factual narrative description. The sole exception being the decidedly pataphysical *Third Law of Coincidence*, drafted in the heat of the moment the day before the conclusion of the events now being retold. The Third Law of Coincidence, briefly stated, argues that: 'All coincident moments will be indicative of a notable concurrence of events, suggestive of possessing a resemblant causal interconnection irrespective of whether this is imaginary or actual.'

It should come as no surprise to discover that, following the events of the previous thirty-six hours, our *dérive* protagonist had now all but abandoned the investigations being conducted in response to the *Driftnet* and had set out in search of what to all intents must have appeared the impossible. Upon reflection I suppose the tone of my narrative must have already prepared the reader for the discovery made that evening. The navigator in question was by now using every available technique he possessed in order to locate playing cards, and in such circumstances their discovery must become more likely. It took another full day – the remnants of yesterday being interrupted by persistent reflection – but for the card discovered to be the anxiously sought after five of diamonds is the type of event that the gestating *Third Law of Coincidence* now thrives upon for its verification.

The card was discovered half obscured amongst a collection of left-footed shoes and other discarded items of clothing long since left behind on the traces of St Andrew's labyrinthine lanes. Criss-crossing the floor of the psychogeographical arena beyond the Church's East wall, the tightly interweaving cobbled surfaces were all that remained of one of Glasgow's densest urban quarters. The fact that the card in question was found at twilight, lying face up, should not, I believe, be of any relevance to the intensity of the phenomenon being investigated.

With both the three and the four already tucked away inside his jacket pocket, our incredulous adventurer immediately headed for the Mitre, a small snug of a bar just off Argyll Street and the agreed rendezvous for those intent on our various evening activities. Walking quickly along the darkening backstreets behind the Tron his only goal was to share the marvel of the discovery. The possibilities of finding another playing card, let alone the five of diamonds, had been casually discussed the previous evening, but no one, not even our protagonist, had seriously contemplated its realisation. (It must be remembered here that a *dérive* is never undertaken with the expectation of fulfilling its original premise, but rather of experiencing its natural evolution – of drifting away from the moment of departure in anticipation of the unknown quality of the point of arrival.) Needless to say, following his demonstration of the three cards in the Mitre that evening, the events now being related become almost the only topic of discussion amongst the members of the section, their various associates, friends and collaborators.

The proven integrity of the individual who had made the discoveries fortunately ensured that the debate centred mainly around the nature of coincidence and the consequences of its accidental encounter; the factual content of the discoveries was never brought into question. (The sole exception being that of one canny individual who suggested that half of those present at yesterday evening's session must have spent a good part of the afternoon planting a number of fives of diamonds around the city.) However – although it was the unfolding of the events leading up to the discovery of each card and the role they played in directing or influencing the consequential behaviour of the protagonist that occupied the majority of the discussion – the most potent observation, made quite early on in the evening, was that there lay within this episode the beginnings of a quite remarkable game of Urban Poker.

The hypothesis went as follows:

Two or more drift teams, containing between one and half a dozen navigators, would begin at a given point in time to search for found playing cards. The cards would naturally have to be the genuine 'unsolicited object' (in Breton's sense of the word), although dishonesty in regard of such matters would be left, as is only natural, to the subjective nature of the individual(s) concerned. Initially each team would seek five cards, a number of which (to be decided between the teams in advance) would then be burned, or in other words discarded. Once this agreed number had then been refound, the hand would be brought to a close and publicly declared, e.g. Full House, Pair, Ace High, etc., the winning team being the one with the best hand.

Almost the moment the last words of this explanation had been uttered, the ensemble gathered together erupted in a spontaneous chorus of approval, suggestion, variation and counterproposal. The idea had definitely taken hold, but then again once the mind had begun to explore the possible consequences then so it should have. And this was precisely what our navigator had begun to do. His inquisitive nature had already started speculating as to how to encourage the evolution of this newly emergent *dérive* ever since the jubilation of picking up the five had begun to fade away. Even while returning from St Andrew's, cards in hand, our navigator had entertained the notion that an alternative set of moves would now be required.

Lets face it, the actual discovery of a six had never stood a chance and any attempt even to begin searching for it had been discarded from the outset. Even the most cursory of calculations posited the chances of success at $1/(55)^4$ – or roughly one in about 9 million – and even that calculation clearly ignored a whole host of other variables. Somehow, the impossibility of discovering the five had contained within it the consciously understood knowledge of the chance of success, and it was that glimpse of the possible that had enabled the card to be sought – not necessarily found, but definitely looked for. With the introduction of the idea of a game of Urban Poker it appeared that this necessary redirecting of the *dérive* had begun.

So as the commotion in the bar subsided, it was our navigator, closely followed by the originator of the idea, who were seen to move away towards the back of the room. Their intention was to transcribe the contents of the conversation, to put everything down on paper before it was passed over and eventually forgotten. (Sadly enough it would not have been the first time that such a brainwave had been allowed to slip away into the mists of an ever-fading memory.) Between the two of them each proposal was considered, analysed and either rejected or co-opted into what was rapidly becoming a coherent ludic structure. Time passed by and the evening seemed to slip away quickly. The conversation ebbed with the pennies that had fuelled it until finally the last half heavy brought our two conspirators back to the agenda at hand: the midnight excursion into Bremner's basement and the first group penetration of the *Inside Outside*. The *Inside Outside* was a Victorian backstreet 'time warp', a spatial ambience that had been completely entombed for well over a century. It had recently been exposed by a local surveying company who, after months of trying to understand the building's complex maze of walls, floors, tunnels and basements, had finally got around to prizing open the various light wells and air shafts concealed inside.

As the dawn light welcomed the following morning, a host of entirely external circumstances now prevented our navigator from pursuing any further *dérive* activity – a state of affairs that would last well into Thursday afternoon. The chain of events immediately surrounding the discovery of the cards appeared to have been broken. In fact it wasn't until the following Wednesday, after a chance encounter the previous evening between the protagonist and the originator, that further progress was to be made. The two of them had agreed to meet up, appropriately enough considering the nature of the subject matter in hand, on the desolate, overgrown island in the middle of the Port Dundas canal loop. This now partially forested waste ground, previously one of Glasgow's busiest ports, was only accessible by climbing precariously along the undercarriage of the single bridge that connected the island with the surrounding area. The gates, side fence and various security bars were not only physically inaccessible, but liberally covered with a malevolent anti-climb paint. No one, however, had the foresight to imagine that an attempt to gain access to the island would be made via the underside of the bridge!

The crossing took about twenty minutes, but once ashore both of them headed immediately for the south side of the island, to a concrete jetty immediately beyond which, just below the surface of the water, lay a rusted wreck of a car with the word 'joker' sprayed across the roof. It was in this setting that the two of them had decided to draft – not conclusively, but sufficient enough for the inaugural game to commence – *The Rules of Urban Poker.*

Despite remaining as close as possible to the original hypothesis, a number of variations upon the initial theme were agreed. The first, and definitely the most interesting, was that the game should be undertaken between different cities. The playing off of one urban entity against another, and the possible transprogrammatic consequences offered by the circumstantial spatial juxtapositioning involved, had evoked considerable enthusiasm. Without concretely appreciating what this might eventually entail, both of them were convinced of its future potential. A game of five-card stud was started on 7 June 1996 between WNLA London, 391 Paris, FluxAlba and Beirut F-ART, with the specific aim of developing these possibilities.

A decision was also made to underline firmly the fact that the cards were not to be deliberately sought. If Breton's criteria for the *objet insolite* were to be held to then the cards would have to give themselves both willingly and unexpectedly to the players of the game. Our navigator had already expressed the opinion that the actual search for the five, as opposed to its discovery, had not been entirely satisfactory and that had he not found anything that day it would have been an extremely frustrating experience. It was his view that an unexpected chance encounter and the sudden reaquaintance of the participant with the ongoing game – despite the obvious increase in game duration – would prove far more satisfying.

Thirdly, it was agreed that rather than various drift teams, a single individual, operating in each city, would lend the game a more distinctly interpersonal character. It's not that teams of individuals in each city were considered erroneous, rather it was more a case of the Glasgow section's relations with other cities at that time involving only individuals, as opposed to groupings, who would be likely to play the game. More pertinent, however, was that our navigating protagonist, after finding three cards of such quality in so short a space of time, was determined to complete the task of locating his hand alone, and that in such circumstances it would be appropriate to pit his discoveries against those made by other like-minded individuals. Team attempts were perfectly plausible for future games, but with this one already half-completed by a single individual, its essence should be maintained.

The only other real change to the original theme was that, rather than waiting until the first five cards had been located, each find should be communicated directly to the opponent(s) involved; the reason being that this would intensify the sense of ongoing participation with the overall unfolding of the game. It was suggested that such a move might encourage dishonesty, but with this question having already been resolved by the decision to accept the word of all participating navigators right from the outset, the suggestion was held to be irrelevant. And so, with continuity of participation being held to be far more important than the irritable subjectivity of apparent truth, the only course of action was to let the game commence.

Previously issued as a privately circulated pamphlet.

DRIFTING: SOME JOURNEYS FOLLOWED
Dominic Paterson

As you walk along, you find things. I think that's the advantage of walking. It's just one of the reasons why I do that a lot. You find things by the wayside or you buy a brochure written by a local historian, which is in a tiny little museum somewhere, which you would never find in London. And in that you find odd details which lead you somewhere else, and so it's a form of unsystematic searching... And the more I got on, the more I felt that, really, one can find something only in that way, i.e. in the same way in which, say, a dog runs through a field. If you look at a dog following the advice of his nose, he traverses a patch of land in a completely unplottable manner. And he invariably finds what he is looking for.

— WG Sebald, The Emergence of Memory [1]

1)
Following the example of Stina Wirfelt, I try to follow the *dérive* described in 'The Joker'; I wander through the version of Glasgow as it appears in Google Earth, January 2011. 'The Joker' describes a series of chance discoveries of playing cards, prompting the idea of 'urban poker' being played across cities and across time. I wonder if any of the magical coincidences described in the essay can be found in the digital realm and whether my present could be linked to that past.
Beginning at the Theatre Royal on Hope Street, I head for the stage door, but there is little trace of any litter, let alone playing cards—or at least there wasn't on 11 May 2009, the day when

---

1   Ed. Lynne Sharon Schwartz, *The Emergence of Memory: conversations with WG Sebald*, New York: Seven Stories, 2007, p. 94.

these images were taken. Portakabins and a city council bin evidence processes of rebuilding and maintenance, rather than the charmed contingencies which link the drifting psychogeographer with the object cast adrift by circumstance. Undeterred, I press on, tracking the various locations described in 'The Joker'.

I soon discover some sites are simply inaccessible or invisible due to Google Earth's reliance on car-mounted cameras: the pedestrian's city eludes its surveillance. But as a resident of Glasgow, I know some of the places have changed or vanished since 1994. The Mitre bar, for instance, is now boarded-up and graffiti-covered. Its iconic neon sign has been displaced to Tontine Lane, where it makes a melancholy pendant to Douglas Gordon's neon work *Empire*. The 'inside-outside' space of Bremner's department store (memorably described by the anonymous author of 'The Joker' as a Victorian backstreet 'time warp') has ceded its place to the more contemporary face of commercial regeneration. If all this makes it difficult to follow in the footsteps of the urban drifter, whose *dérives* necessarily head off the beaten track, so too does the camera's vantage point make it impossible to look down at the ground. The fragments and ephemera that offer fleeting traces of contemporary life to the psychogeographer barely register in the digital urban landscape. Outside The Griffin pub, near where the four of diamonds was apparently found, I scour the street for any equivalent *objet trouvé,* but all I can see is a warped road surface reminiscent of a futurist painting on which the only thing legible is a territorial claim: ©2009 Google.

As I 'walk' along the virtual Sauchiehall Street towards The Griffin, I notice that the traffic seems to move backwards down the street as I progress westwards along it. The images were, it seems, taken from the rear of a vehicle heading east, so that the forward movement imaged on my computer screen makes a movement backwards in time. There is a short flurry, a leap through time, a blurring, and then a gradual resolution. I am reminded of Walter Benjamin's famous reading of Paul Klee's *Angelus Novus* as the angel of history: "His face is turned towards the past. Where a chain of events appears before *us, he* sees one single catastrophe, which keeps piling wreckage upon wreckage and hurls it at his feet".[2] The comparison is admittedly not exact; Benjamin's angel faces the past but is perpetually driven forward into the future, while Google Earth celebrates nothing so much as the idea of being able to move in any direction, free of bodily constraints, regardless of which way the wind blows. The wreckage of history is hard to discern in this world in which, uncannily, the city always appears in the clear light of day.

Benjamin repeatedly wrote of the city as a collision of temporalities and histories. In those 'inside outsides' of the Parisian arcades, the glass-covered shopping streets (of which Glasgow too has examples), he found archaic dream worlds which combined past, present and future. Benjamin's own relationship to such dream worlds might be modelled as a combination of the ways in which such archetypal characters as the *flâneur*, the ragpicker, and the collector, viewed, gathered, and rehabilitated what they could of the city. Like the *flâneur*, Benjamin was itinerant, he too was capable of harnessing distraction as a mode of attention; like the ragpicker he was an accumulator of the overlooked, the obsolete, the abandoned; and like the collector, he conferred meaning and value on objects so that subjective passion outweighed utility as a source of value. In this materialist apprehension of urban modernity, a tactile, intimate knowledge of things plays a crucial part; the reveries of the wandering *flâneur* need the corrective of the downward gaze of the ragpicker. These modes of relating to the city and its embedded historical traces constitute what Benjamin conceptualised as practices of 'innervation', ways of handling the shocks of modernity by absorbing them at a bodily as well as a psychological level.

Gambling *(hasardspiel)* is one of a number of forms of play that Benjamin thought of as exemplifying such innervations. It was with reference to the possibility of a utopian transform of such play that Benjamin invested cinema (*Lichtspiele*) with high hopes, as Miriam Hansen explains:

---

2   Walter Benjamin, 'On the Concept of History', *Selected Writings*, vol. 4, 1938–1940, London: Belknap, 2006, p. 392.

The rare gift of proper gambling, pursued—and mis-
used—by individuals in a hermetically isolated manner
and for private gain, becomes a model of mimetic
innervation for a collective that seems to have all but lost,
literally, its senses; which lacks that bodily presence of
mind that could yet "turn the threatening future into a
fulfilled 'now'"...Benjamin wagers that the only chance
for a collective, nondestructive, playful innervation of
technology rests with the new mimetic technologies of film
and photography—notwithstanding their ongoing uses
to the contrary. As early as 1927, Siegfried Kracauer had
designated the turn to the photographic media as the "go-
for-broke game" (*Vabanque-Spiel*) of history. By 1936, the
political crisis had forced the literary intellectual himself
into the role of a gambler, making his play, as it were, in
the face of imminent catastrophe.[3]

If gambling is a private accommodation with fate, then Benjamin
gambled on film as a collective grasping of history, as something
more than a space of reverie in images. Cardsharps knew the
advantages of the tactile over the purely visual—from at least
the 16th century they were marking playing cards by pricking
or punching them, leaving traces that deft fingers could follow
and read.[4] As with those unfortunate gamblers caught out by
such sharp practice, Benjamin's dream of a cinema of innervation
was perhaps always going to end in disappointment, the odds
stacked against it from the start. But film can at least perhaps,
like the ragpicker pouring over the streets, or the *flâneur* or
psychogeographer wandering through them, grasp the play
of lost futures and vanishing pasts which animates the city's
historical layers. The advent of digital worlds such as Google
Earth simultaneously brings those layers closer, making them

3   Miriam Bratu Hansen, 'Room-for-play: Benjamin's Gamble with
Cinema', *October*, vol. 109, Summer 2004, pp. 10–11.

4   Jonathan Allen, 'Mark of Integrity', *Cabinet*, no. 33, Spring
2009, pp. 61–65.

viewable and searchable, while also removing them ever more firmly from the sphere of action.

To *dérive* via computer screen is to wander through historical layers embedded in images. But might it also be a space to forget where you are, to lose track of time, to focus your senses almost entirely in the field of vision? And, in so doing, to possibly ignore the hand that history has dealt, to be unable to pick it up, turn it over and weigh up its potential?

2)

When he was writing his *Reveries of the Solitary Walker* Jean-Jacques Rousseau made a note on the back of a playing card: "My whole life has been little else than a long reverie divided into chapters by my daily walks".[5] This observation would seem to provide the structure of the *Reveries* themselves: ten chapters describing ten walks, in which Rousseau's thoughts continually wander from the natural world to philosophical or biographical matters and back again.

In the 'Second Walk', he describes a journey made on Thursday 24 October 1776 from his home in the Rue Plâtrière, out along the boulevards to Rue du Chemin-Vert and the hills of Ménilmontant, towards the village of Charonne, a route which takes him through "vineyards and meadows" and a "charming stretch of countryside".[6] Encounters with the natural world along this route spur reflections on fate, destiny and mortality. At first Rousseau's discovery of rare flowers pleases him greatly, but the melancholic autumnal scene in which these flowers are embedded prompts him to compare himself to the landscape, with winter approaching and "with a soul still full of intense feelings and a mind still adorned with a few flowers, even if they were already

5   Jean-Jacques Rousseau, *Reveries of the Solitary Walker,* trans. Peter France, London: Penguin, 2004, p. 12.

6   Ibid, p. 36.

blighted by sadness and withered with care".[7] These thoughts
blossom into a recollection of the journey made by the writer's
soul from childhood to old age, something Rousseau describes as
becoming pleasurable.

The reverie is rudely interrupted when a Great Dane knocks
the philosopher to the ground and he passes out. On regaining
consciousness, Rousseau claims, he knows neither where nor
who he is, but is elated, as if born again. The 'Second Walk'
doesn't dwell long in this innocent state, and Rousseau ends the
chapter hounded by thoughts of conspiracies against him and
his reputation. Though the effort to connect and interpret what
seem to be mere chance occurrences exhausts him, Rousseau is
convinced that "the accumulation of so many chance circumstances … is too extraordinary to be a mere coincidence".[8]

What Rousseau fears above all is that there is a conspiracy that
will destroy his reputation after his death. Follow the route
of the 'Second Walk' route now, however, through the virtual
streets of Paris, and you will begin on what has been renamed
the Rue Jean-Jacques Rousseau. You will also and find that the
pastoral scene described has been supplanted by the cemetery
of Père Lachaise and by the inexorable expansion of the city.
"Everything is in a constant flux on this earth," Rousseau
writes, "nothing keeps the same unchanging shape, and our af-
fections, being attached to things outside us, necessarily change
and pass away as they do. Always out ahead of us or lagging
behind, they recall a past which is gone or anticipate a future
which may never come into being".[9] Perhaps cities are the exemplary sites in which our desire to find fixed coordinates
amongst the historical flux plays itself out. The renaming of the
Rue Plâtrière after its famously itinerant inhabitant might mark
one such attempt to anchor the present in a past that is itself
unstable.

---

7   Ibid, p. 37.

8   Ibid, p. 44.

9   Ibid, p. 88.

3)
The many dramatic changes Paris has undergone since the eighteenth century might seem to entrench the *Reveries* firmly in their period, as if the world they describe has been washed away by the flux Rousseau describes. However, the literary trope the reveries help establish—the walk as a textual space of revelatory reverie—has proven remarkably resilient. In his extraordinary novel *The Rings of Saturn*, WG Sebald elides the act of walking with an associative mental wandering that doubles as historical reverie in which the present seamlessly cedes to other times and places. Part VII of the book provides a vivid example of this.[10] It opens with the narrator standing on Dunwich Heath in Suffolk at midday. The vista provokes the narrator to reflect on the human interventions which formed that landscape, especially the deforestation begun by the very first settlers of the region, and later continued to supply shipbuilding and fuel the smelting of iron. Sebald's narrator follows this passage with an account of his disorientation on Dunwich Heath, with its uniform covering of purple heather, its signposts which "gave no directions to any place or its distance", and its labyrinthine pathways. The text releases the narrator from this labyrinth only to plunge back into it in a dream of the maze at nearby Somerleyton Hall. This maze is in turn transformed, so that the dreamer comes to recognise it as a cross-section of his brain. Then the dream changes again, into an apocalyptic vision of a disintegrating landscape at night. Like the book from which it comes, the whole section describes a kind of labyrinthine spiralling through place and memory, history and imagination. This spiralling, with its tangential connections and leaps of time and place, allegorises the journeys made by the imagination of the writer in his study, and by the reader wherever they might enter the book. Here, as in the virtual space of Google Earth, all kinds of connections can be made, any distances covered; we can pass from history into reverie and back again without being sure as to where the borders lie.
Sebald speculates that we all might "lose our sense of reality to

10   WG Sebald, *The Rings of Saturn*, London: Harvill, 1998.

the precise degree to which we are engrossed in our own work, and perhaps that is why we see in the increasing complexity of our mental constructs a means for greater understanding, even while intuitively we know that we shall never be able to fathom the imponderables that govern our course through life". Despite such doubts, coincidence is never meaningless in Sebald's writing; it is revealing, both of the historical contingencies formative of our world, and of the desires we follow even when engaged in unsystematic searching. Here, it differs from navigating within the virtual world: rather than a space in which one moves in a continuous present imaged from the past (doing so in a way that one's own body and its time get lost even as the world appears perfectly mapped), Sebald's wanderings offer a different way of getting lost or losing oneself, in which something of value can be found or recovered from unmappable domains.

4)

The famed psychogeographical and situationist *dérives* of the 1950s and 60s are akin to Sebald's literary wandering—the terrain they traverse is, above all, historical. Guy Debord describes drifting east through Paris with an accomplice on 6 March 1956, and unintentionally ending up amid the "repulsive petit-bourgeois landscape" of the Eleventh arrondissement.[11] The only relief from the commercial uniformity of the location comes, Debord recounts, in their chance encounter with a storefront at 160 Rue Oberkampf bearing the legend 'Delicatessen-provisions A. Breton'. Doubtless the fact that this discovery recalled Breton's own fateful chance encounters on the streets of Paris, and the wanderings described in his novel *Nadja* (1928), added to the delicious irony of the moment for Debord. However, as Simon Sadler has rightfully emphasised, the surrealist deployment of chance was reactionary in Debord's eyes, and something he wished to clearly differentiate from situationist *dérives*.

Another incident from the *dérive* of 6 March 1956: Debord's

---

11   Guy Debord, 'Two Accounts of the Dérive', trans. Thomas Y Levin, *Les Lèvres Nues*, no. 9, November 1956.

excursion comes to its end at Place de Stalingrad, with the unexpected and incongruous sight of Claude-Nicholas Ledoux's 1786 tollhouse rotunda. Debord describes it as:

> A virtual ruin left in an incredible state of abandonment, whose charm is singularly enhanced by the curve of the elevated subway line that passes by at close distance ... One should no doubt liken this to the clearly psychogeographic appeal of the illustrations found in books for very young schoolchildren; here, for didactic reasons, one finds collected in a single image a harbor, a mountain, an isthmus, a forest, a river, a dike, a cape, a bridge, a ship, and an archipelago. Claude Lorrain's images of harbors are not unrelated to this procedure.[12]

In making seemingly unlikely connections and superimpositions, Debord proposes a way of unearthing the layers of history buried in the eternal rationalist present implied by Ledoux's architecture. Anyone with a computer and an internet connection can follow Debord's itinerary, and view the play of curves he describes. But what is really worth following is the way that this chance discovery of the abandoned tollhouse trigger connections which question the 'naturalness' of its form and its presence in the city, and thus expose the forces which have left it stranded in history. In 1957 Ralph Rumney, the lone member of the London Psychogeographical Association, proposed to make a psycho-geographical map of Venice. Rumney recalls, "the town lent itself perfectly to such an exercise because of its labyrinthine nature. And the thing that struck me most was that when people go to San Marco, they are encouraged to look at the mosaics above their heads. In my case, maybe because I have a slightly hunched back or for whatever reason, I looked at the ground".[13] Like the author of 'The Joker', Rumney had his eyes trained on

---

12   Ibid.

13   Ralph Rumney, *The Consul* (trans. Malcolm Imrie), London: Verso, 2002, p. 47.

the traces left beneath his feet. But his failure to produce the map on time led to his expulsion from the situationist group. Debord announced this in a text published in the first issue of *Internationale Situationiste*, which ironises Rumney's status as a man missing in action:

> Heavy were the losses among those explorers of old to whom we owe our understanding of objective geography. We must expect casualties, too, among the new seekers of social space ... Thus it is that the Venetian jungle has shown itself to be the stronger, closing over a young man full of life and promise, who is now lost to us, a mere memory among so many others.[14]

---

14   Ibid, p. 56.

The Mitre Bar, Glasgow, 1990s. Photo: Alan Dimmick

A CONVERSATION

Stina Wirfelt and Deborah Stratman

STINA WIRFELT: I'm republishing 'The Joker' text I sent to you. It works as an analogy of the way I'd like to work, especially in relation to my last video, *Tame Time* (2010), which creates a fictional narrative in response to a place.

DEBORAH STRATMAN: The text also reminded me of *The Village Wash* (2006), the film you made as a student. You've always had a consistent interest in concurrence and coincidence—the objects or events that become holes, punching through one experience of reality, and providing a window to another concurrent narrative, location or history.

SW: 'The Joker' constructs a story out of random experiences by applying a structure that the random pieces fit into. This is a method I use in my work too.

DS: When I was reading it I wondered if you ever thought to yourself, "I find playing cards all the time when I'm walking around"?

SW: No, I wish! I don't think I nurture my inner mystic enough. I should pay more attention to all these 'signs' around me. But there is a funny story behind my search for 'The Joker'. I started looking into the concept of psychogeography when I was working on *Tame Time*. I hadn't heard much about it or the Situationists previously, so it felt like a big discovery. I read about the Workshop for Non Linear Architecture (WNLA) on the internet and was immediately interested when I saw they had a section based in Glasgow. I found out that 'The Joker' was printed in an anthology by Stewart Home. His anthology was out of print, so I tracked down a reference copy at the National Libraries of Scotland and went across to Edinburgh to read it. I was curious about the anonymous author of this text, particularly because Glasgow's a small city. Since graduating, I've spent a huge amount of time thinking through context and how to place myself in a history of work. I started asking around a little bit and eventually tracked the author down and made contact to see if he would be willing to be interviewed about the WNLA's activities back then.

DS: When you say "back then", how long ago is that?

SW: The mid 1970s. It is a funny time gap as well: the feeling of recent history. I'm quite interested in the nineties at the moment.

DS: It hasn't really stepped into revival yet.

SW: The author told me he'd decided to not make any more comments about WNLA because he was suspended by the group after publishing this very text.

DS: Oh really? Suspended?

SW: WNLA was very anti-publicity. It's like the opposite approach of the company of architects working on the Commonwealth Games now, for instance. The latter are trying to write the future beforehand, whereas WNLA are doing their best to erase the past.

DS: Or perhaps the present? Like brushing away your footsteps as you walk.

SW: I can appreciate the gesture of doing that in your artistic practice, but it also felt like I was shut out of very interesting work. 'The Joker' mentions The Mitre, a pub that is now closed and boarded up. Selfridges bought the whole block around that area to build a massive store and then abandoned its plans, but the bar is still gone. Just standing outside of the boarded up pub I had this profound experience of being left out of things that I wanted to be part of.

DS: Does this group still meet or is it long finished?

SW: I think it was very temporary, and some of the members have probably left Glasgow. I don't even know how many activities they did. But I find it interesting how myths are created as time pass. In a way, trying to erase the past makes the myth of the group stronger.

DS: I wonder what was behind the distrust of 'The Joker'. Did WNLA think it provided too much of a singular map while it wanted multiple maps of its past, or was it about the writing?

SW: The author didn't expand on it. I imagine WNLA wanted to do something truly temporal, something purely experienced by the people who were doing it at the time. I can see why, but the effect is the opposite. I'm often more curious when I'm denied these details.

DS: 'The Joker' is like the wall that appears to the narrator in *Tame Time*. The film's narrator talks about the wall representing the present and that it prevents her seeing the future being built behind it. The wall is a physical object plonked into the course of time and she has to negotiate the wall as a marker, like the text is for you. Both these things are supposed to keep you out, but it makes you more curious about what's behind it. There is a phrase in 'The Joker' I love: it describes a touristic walkway as "a negative psychogeographic sink". It's exciting to know there are charged psychogeographical areas, while others that are neutered of any potential interest. I remember my obsession with this idea when I was making *In Order Not To Be Here* (2002), a film shot entirely in suburbs and corporate parks. I was interested in these sites for precisely that reason: they had a hollowness devoid of any potential oracular or spiritual quality—they are gutted of these things. I was curious about the woman speaking in *Tame Time*. Is her monologue entirely scripted, or did you base it on a character that you know?

SW: No, it's entirely scripted but I had a very specific character in mind. The voice of the narrator is very close to the person that I was imagining. I was looking for someone interested in acting, and the lady I found does amateur dramatics and lives close to the area featured in *Tame Time*. People often assume that this is her story, which perhaps has to do with her way of reading and the sound of her voice. But I initially wrote the script with the voice in mind and went on to find it—it was a lucky shot.

DS: Her voice is very conversational, observational.

SW: I cast the character as a dog walker because in the spaces I was shooting the only other people I ran into were dog walkers. If a dead body turns up somewhere it's almost always found by a dog walker. Dog walkers are always negotiating these forgotten places—even on Google Streetview, they're there.

DS: When I watch your film it seems like Glasgow is like a mini Beijing. Everything is in flux, under construction, decaying. There is a sense of a city in permanent transition, and your films focus on spots where that is particularly evident. Your navigation of Google Streetview shows arrows super-imposed onto locations, how seasons suddenly change if you just go one block over, or how a structure might appear that wasn't there before. I wonder about the technologies that make or predict time and how radically they can shift the paradigm of how we perceive time and space. This is related to film editing—the sense of interruption, and how one reality can interrupt and insert itself into another. Looking at your practice, I was wondering if that is something of direct influence, or maybe it is just subliminally influential?

SW: I've spent a lot of time on Google Streetview, going to places I have and haven't visited in the real world. It has a fundamental effect on the perception space and time because it sets out to map space, although it also inadvertently maps time in a really awkward but visually seamless way.

DS: You appear to be looking for different technologies that concern linkage or porosity, whereas I'm a creature of habit and get really wrapped up in patterns. I set myself up to go to a place where I can't rely on familiar tools like language or culture. I have to be open to observe and experience something. My senses are wide open in those moments.

SW: Being observational in that way, throwing yourself into a completely new situation, is quite different from seeing something regularly, maybe everyday, and noticing the small shifts in the patterns.

DS: That's true. I'm certainly less good at doing it in my everyday life. I need to intentionally set-up, to stumble on something. I'd like to be the kind of person who, even though I bike the same route to work every day, would be able to see something or appreciate something new.

SW: I find it hard to respond to a new situation, I need the repetition. When I think of your travels and the projects that you've done abroad, it seems like you've been going out searching for something very specific before you head out there.

DS: Sometimes I go searching but sometimes the searching is just a McGuffin. It sounds utopian, but it's true: if you're looking you'll find something. Maybe you've had this experience too: you don't entirely know the intention while you're shooting material, but during the gathering process you hit upon a link, story, or person. The puzzle pieces come together later. And other times I might go out with more specific intentions, "I need a shot of X", and I search until I find that thing. There are these two different modes of working.

SW: I identify with both in my work but I'm more interested in this first way of working because it's a way of discovering through making the film. The film can become the documentation of my realisation of something. The difficulty is that the gathering phase could go on forever.

DS: Right, indefinitely!

SW: And you could just end up with a huge pile of unconnected material.

DS: That is how I worked when I first started making films—it was pure collection, to the point where I had no idea why I was shooting. It wasn't until a decade later probably that I became more comfortable in sensing a whole in the structure, going out finding the shots to fill the holes. I think about this in relation to *Tame Time*, and whether the location or the story came first?

SW: I'd made *Monuments* (2008), an earlier film in that same area. The site I photographed for that film is now where the Athletes Village is under construction for the Commonwealth Games. When I took the photographs I realised they would become a historical document, so

I wanted to go back and do something, and yet I was completely in the dark about what would come of it. I just started filming, spending time there. I knew from the start that I wanted to make a fictional narrative rather than an essay, primarily because of fiction's power to suck in a viewer.

DS: In my film *O'er The Land* (2009), I've noticed the audience's body shifts when storytelling begins. I can see it physically reflected in people's bodies: they change their type of attention. I'm a storyteller, but I don't necessarily speak with words. I've never felt particularly equipped to write narratives or voice-overs but I do use snippets of found stories. Even though you're interested in storytelling, *Tame Time* really starts from geography. The location was the fertilising ground, or the decomposed ground where you planted your seed. I, too, often start from a place or an interest in geography. The location catalyses the story and events. In the words of Michael Snow, events take place, they literally take it. The way that land or places can harbour stories has always been a natural way for me to think about them.

SW: Where was the starting point for *O'er The Land*?

DS: I don't remember. It probably came out of projects that were looking at fear and the way that we determine who we are through our nationalistic habits. I read a quote by a pizzeria owner who questioned what we lose in the name of freedom. We use the word 'freedom' all the time, we paste it on anything to make it okay. 'Freedom' is even used to absolve military aggression. It took a while for me to figure out if I felt okay with making a film about such a broad subject. It was intimidating, but in the end I guess I was interested in iconography and heroics, and how nations rely on these to feel a sense of personal history on a national level. At some point during the film, the whole history of manifest destiny and expansionism became entwined with the plot. I was interested in how freedom for Americans, or the concept of it, is complexly tangled up with ownership and material property: if you own things you need to defend them. As soon as the concept of owning material things (and the need to defend them) is sutured with the idea of freedom then I wonder how it can still represent freedom. O'er the land asks questions but doesn't really give you answers. It operates as a mirror: it reflects viewer's pre-existing ideas around freedom. People read into the film's images and sequences based on what they already bring to the film. I didn't want the film to be a dogmatic defence of what freedom should be; I wanted to present a philosophical questioning of why this word has become glue that holds the diverse ideas of Americanism together.

SW: I view the film in the context of recent wars. That is what I see in the mirror, the militarisation. Perhaps it's a consequence of the idea of freedom because, as you say, it is so linked to ownership and seems completely detached to taking any responsibility for the consequences.

DS: It reminds me of the saying, "if you're carrying an armload of hammers, every problem starts to look like a nail". To some degree, the film was a response to my own exasperation with that condition. There is a very palpable ratcheting-up of militarisation that happens in the film. You see increasingly technologised versions of defence. In the beginning, it's just guys walking in a forest with their little guns, and at the end you see a B2 and flame throwers. The film is a product of the times I live in.

SW: Do you rely on certain interpersonal skills to gain access to all these almost closed societies, which comprise men in many cases?

DS: A big part of the process is knowing that people like to be listened to, that they want to know people are interested in what they're saying. If you come to some Viet-Cong re-enactors at a machine gun festival and tell them you are interested in how people define freedom, they want to talk about it! In America the right to bear guns, to own guns, is how a lot of people define freedom. I am purposefully opaque, though. I don't say where I'm coming from, partly because I don't know entirely where I am coming from, but also because I want to get the widest range of responses possible. I'm not intimidating, I don't make people nervous. You probably know that if you're a woman carrying a camera, people tend to think you're making a home movie. When we were shooting *The BLVD* (1999), my friend J had the same camera as me. People would always ask him what news channel he was working for. People don't ascribe the same authority to a woman with a camera—they're less guarded. In many cases, that works to my advantage.

SW: In the UK, it's getting more and more difficult to get permission to film in public spaces. I can't tell you how many times I've been turned away as a security threat. Once I was filming in a huge shopping centre in a town that neighbours Glasgow. I had only just got the camera up on the tripod when a man approached me and told me I wasn't allowed to film. I managed to find another security guard and begged him to let me record. He said he would speak to his boss and told me to stay where I was. I stood there knowing that they were watching me on the CCTV determining whether I was a risk or not. It's an awkward phenomenon that we are all constantly being filmed but don't have the right to do it ourselves.

DS: The camera is equated with control and authority. It's the same idea of entering a building with guns everywhere; if you walk in with a gun you're a threat, an infiltrator. I got caught red-handed when I was shooting *In order not to be here* (2002). I was shooting in malls and parking lots, always spaces that would be the quickest to notice my presence. In places of commercial activity security guards are right on it. One guy actually gave me a little card with rules of what you could and couldn't do on the premises. One of them expressly said you couldn't "engage in creative activity that does not propagate consumption". They actually name it on there! You can't be creative unless it provokes people to buy things.

EMMA WOLUKAU-WANAMBWA
WITH KATE DAVIS,
LIS RHODES, JUDITH WILLIAMSON AND
PAULINE BOUDRY / RENATE LORENZ

(THE WORKING TITLE IS
NOT YET KNOWN)

A CURRENCY OF SIGNS
Judith Williamson

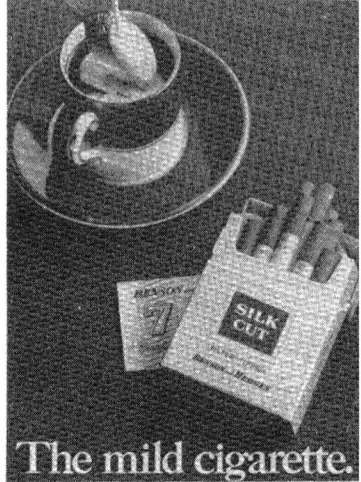

A4

A4 Connecting an object with an object: This is perfectly simple: the colours of the cigarette packet are exactly those of the cup of coffee—white and maroon; and there is even a hint of gold on the rim of the packet's lid, matching the rim of the cup and saucer. The assumption here is that because the containers are the same (in terms of colour) the products have the same qualities: here, primarily mildness, though also a slight suggestion of richness. The cup of coffee acts as an 'objective correlative' (cf. section b) for the quality invoked.

A5 Connecting an object and a world: Here, the colours—black and white, with a touch of silver—and also the shapes—rectangular, streamlined—connect the cigarette packet to what the ad itself describes as a whole 'world': 'the world of Lambert and Butler'. The visual link between the packet and the world is exaggeratedly apparent: literally everything in the room is black and white and geometrical. However, as the two containers were compared in the last example, here also the correlated objects, packet and world, are in fact containers; the parallel of the cigarettes being, here, not coffee (in matching cup) but people (in matching room). The people are the contents of the room just as are the cigarettes of the packet. Thus the words can be read as relating directly to the people; they are obviously terms usually applied to people and *not* things, yet here, in using them *about* things, they are equating these with people: 'The first of a new generation of distinguished cigarettes [/people] . . . with a quality and style that sets them apart from other cigarettes [/people].' So here the colour correlation brings explicitly into focus a link between the people and the cigarettes that was implicit in the words chosen. There is, however, another sort of reversal here as the packet of cigarettes is, supposedly, an accessory to the distinguished, stylish world depicted, fitting into it visually by colour and style; yet, in naming the *world* after the *cigarettes* ('the world of Lambert and Butler'), and in greatly exaggerating the features of the cigarette box in this physical world, we see that the world and the people are actually an accessory of the product, and not the other way round. Instead of the product being created out of a need in the world, it creates its own world, an exaggerated reflection of itself.

A5

A6 Connecting the object and a person: The product is a whole kitchen, yet here again, the person – a woman – has been made to match it. Her white clothes immediately link her to the slightly open cupboard, whose interior is the only other patch of white in the room. This gives a suggestion of availability. The woman's skin is precisely the same colour as the eggs. Her hair matches the cupboards. Again, we see that while the kitchen is meant to reflect *her*, she is in fact merely an object in the kitchen like one of the copper pans or the eggs or pieces of French bread. No wonder she looks so uncomfortable in it.

A6

A7 *The retinted world of the advertisement:* Finally, a straightforward example just to illustrate the wide use and significance of colour correlations: the product and the world and the woman (the consumer) are all reduced to just two colours (gold and brown)—a typical manipulation or restatement of the world to link it to the two-dimensionality of advertising. This shows very clearly what has been seen in all these ads: a selecting of certain elements, things or people from the ordinary world, and then a rearranging and altering them in terms of a product's myth to create a new world, the world of the advertisement. This is the essence of all advertising: components of 'real' life, our life, are used to speak a new language, the advertisement's. Its language, its terms (here, gold and brown; the 'bronze lustre' message), *are* the myth; for as we have seen, they are too full of coincidence, of colour co-ordination, to be real. The very means of expression (as shown by colour, in this case) is the myth.

A7

Use of colour is simply a *technique*, used primarily in pictorial advertising, to make correlations between a product and other things. Since this book is based on magazine advertisements which are more easily reproduced than those in the cinema or on TV, I have included analyses of ads A2–A7 simply to alert the reader to this technique. The use of colour is not significant in itself; it is the significance of the correlation it makes that forms the basis of my theory. It is important not to confuse the particular properties of the technological medium with the generic properties of advertisements. On the screen, for example, connections are made by cutting, by the reverse field technique (where facing fields of vision are shown alternately), and so on. There is an advertisement for chocolate in cinema intermissions where a girl jumps upwards into the air, and then there is a cut to a bar of chocolate leaping upwards—so that the *movement* is continuous, although the objects are different. The cutting here fills the same correlating function as colour in the preceding ads; what is important is that ads in all media make these connections, *through formal techniques*, not on the level of the overt signified but via the signifiers.

Having established with these examples that such connections are made, I now embark on my theory of *why* they are made, and the significance of *how* they are made.

(a) Differentiation   There is very little real difference between brands of product within any category, such as detergents, margarine, paper towels and so on. Therefore it is the first function of an advertisement to *create* a differentiation between one particular product and others in the same category. It does this by providing the product with an 'image'; this image only succeeds in differentiating between products in so far as *it* is part of a system of differences. The identity of anything depends more on what it is *not* than what it is, since boundaries are primarily distinctions: and there are no 'natural' distinctions between most products. This can be seen by the fact that a *group* of products will sometimes be marketed with the same 'image', in a set or 'range' (cf. A11)—these usually have names, like 'Maybelline' or 'Spring Bouquet' etc.: the limits of identity are chosen arbitrarily, it is clear, because in other cases two identical products from the very same manufacturer will be given different names and different images. If two different bottles of cleansing milk can have the same name—'Outdoor girl' or suchlike, but a third, apparently similar, can appear with a different name and therefore with supposedly different properties, it immediately becomes apparent that there are no

logical boundaries between most products. Surf and Daz essentially contain the same chemicals. Obviously there *are* products with special qualities or particular uses, but these do not usually need extensive advertising campaigns: the bulk of advertising covers exactly the areas where goods are the same: cigarettes, cornflakes, beer, soap.

I am taking a group of perfume advertisements—two of which come from the same manufacturer: these provide a good example of the creation of 'images' since perfumes *can* have no particular significance. This is a type of ad which can give no real information about the product (what information can be given about a smell?) so that the function of differentiation rests totally on making a connection with an image drawn from outside the ad world.

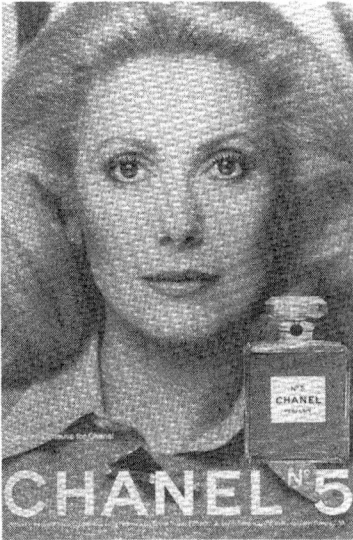

A8

A8: Catherine Deneuve's face and the Chanel bottle are not linked by any narrative, simply by juxtaposition: but there is not supposed to be any *need* to link them directly, they are as it were in apposition in the grammar of the ad, placed together in terms of an *assumption* that they have the same meaning, although the connection is really a random one. For the face and the bottle are not inherently connected: there is no link between Catherine Deneuve *in herself* and Chanel No. 5: but the link is in terms of what Catherine Deneuve's face *means to us*, for this is what Chanel No. 5 is trying to mean to us, too. The advertisement presents this transference of meaning to us as a *fait accompli*, as though it were simply presenting two objects with the same meaning, but in fact it is only *in* the advertisement that this transference takes place. Chanel No. 5 only has the 'meaning' or image that it shares with Catherine Deneuve by having become associated with Catherine Deneuve through this very advertisement. So what Catherine Deneuve's face means to us in the world of magazines and films, Chanel No. 5 seeks to mean and comes to mean in the world of consumer goods. The ad is using another already existing mythological language or sign system, and appropriating a relationship that exists in that system between signifier (Catherine Deneuve) and signified (glamour, beauty) to speak of its product in terms of the same relationship; so that the perfume can be substituted for Catherine Deneuve's face and can also be made to signify glamour and beauty.

Using the structure of one system in order to give structure to another, or to translate the structure of another, is a process which must involve an intermediate structure, a system of systems or 'meta-system' at the point where the translation takes place: this is the advertisement. Advertisements are constantly translating between systems of meaning, and therefore constitute a vast meta-system where values from different areas of our lives are made interchangeable.

Thus the work of the advertisement is not to invent a meaning for No. 5, but to translate meaning for it by means of a sign system we already know. It is only because Catherine Deneuve has an 'image', a significance in one sign system, that she can be used to create a new system of significance relating to perfumes. If she were not a film star and famous for her chic type of French beauty, if she did not *mean* something to us, the link made between her face and the perfume would be meaningless. So it is not her face as such, but its position in a system of signs where it signifies flawless French beauty, which makes it useful as a piece of linguistic currency to sell Chanel.

The system of signs from which the product draws its image is a *referent system* in that the sign lifted out of it and placed in the ad (in this case, Catherine Deneuve's face) *refers back to it*. It is not enough simply to know who Catherine Deneuve is: this will not help you to understand the ad. Someone from another culture who knew that Catherine Deneuve was a model and film star would still not understand the significance of her image here, because they would not have access to the referent system as a whole. And it is only by referring back to this system as a system of *differences* that the sign can function: it is hollow of meaning in itself, its signified is only a distinction rather than a 'content'. Only the form and structure of the referent system are appropriated by the advertisement system; it is the relationship and distinction between parts, rather than the parts themselves, that make an already-structured external system so valuable to advertising. The links made between elements from a referent system and products arise from the *place* these elements have in the whole system rather than from their inherent qualities. Thus Catherine Deneuve has significance only in that she is not, for example, Margaux Hemingway.

A 9

A9 Babe: The 'image' of this ad derives its impact from the existence of precisely such ads as A8, as it is able to 'kick off' against the more sedate Catherine Deneuve image and others like it. This new perfume, 'Babe', has been launched in a campaign using the new 'discovery' Margaux Hemingway. The significance of her novelty, youth and 'Tomboy' style, which has value only *in relation* to the more typically 'feminine' style usually connected with modelling, is carried over to the perfume: which is thus signified as new and 'fresh', in relation to other established perfumes. There would be no significance at all in the fact that Margaux Hemingway is wearing a karate outfit and has her hair tied back to look almost like a man's, were it not that *other* perfume ads show women wearing pretty dresses and with elaborately styled hair. The meaning is not, however, generated *inside* the advertisement system: there is a meaning in terms of 'women's liberation' and 'breaking conventions' in a model's having a tough, 'liberated' image (in one TV ad for 'Babe', Margaux Hemingway mends the car while her boyfriend watches) rather than a passive, 'feminine' one. In the widest

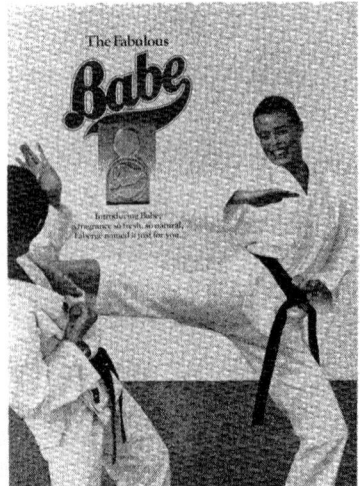

sphere of meaning which the ad draws on, even outside modelling and images, the meaning still depends on a contrast, since the very idea of women doing karate is only significant because most women do *not* and have not done anything of the sort. (See Chapter 8.)

So this advertisement uses the 'Margaux Hemingway' image, *which itself depends for its significance on not being Catherine Deneuve's image* to give 'Babe' a distinct place in the inventory of perfumes, emphasising its novelty (its *not being like* what has gone before) and its difference from all the others. It uses a contrast made in social terms, 'feminine' vs. 'liberated', as signified by two models, to make a contrast between products.

In the mythological system of fashion and publicity Catherine Deneuve and Margaux Hemingway are mutually differentiated and can only have value as signs in relation to each other: as Saussure says: 'in all cases, then, we discover not *ideas* given in advance but *values* emanating from the system. When we say that these values correspond to concepts, it is understood that these concepts are purely differential, not positively defined by their content but negatively defined by their relation with other terms of the system. Their most precise characteristic is that they are what the others are not.'[1] Thus with Catherine Deneuve and Margaux Hemingway it is the *difference* between their significances (taking them not as women but as signs, for this is what they are in this context) that makes them valuable in advertising. Advertisements appropriate the formal relations of pre-existing systems of differences. They use distinctions existing in social mythologies to create distinctions between products: this seems like the reverse of 'totemism', where *things* are used to differentiate groups of people: however the differentiating process in advertisements works in both directions simultaneously. I have only unravelled the elements of this process in order to make the discussion of them clearer, focusing here on the differentiating of products, while 'totemism', differentiating between people, is discussed in the next chapter.

[1] Saussure, *Course in General Linguistics*, quoted in *Saussure* by Jonathan Culler, Fontana, 1976, p. 26.

Extracts from Judith Williamson, *Decoding Advertisements: Ideology and Meaning in Advertising*, 1978, London: Marion Boyars, 1994

TWO CONVERSATIONS, ABRIDGED

Emma Wolukau-Wanambwa with Lis Rhodes (text)
and Kate Davis (image)

From: Kate Davis
Subject: Re:
  Date: 13 January 2011 22:14:24 GMT
    To: Emma Wolukau-Wanambwa

From: Emma Wolukau-Wanambwa
Subject: Re:
Date: 17 January 2011 12:32:15 GMT
To: Kate Davis

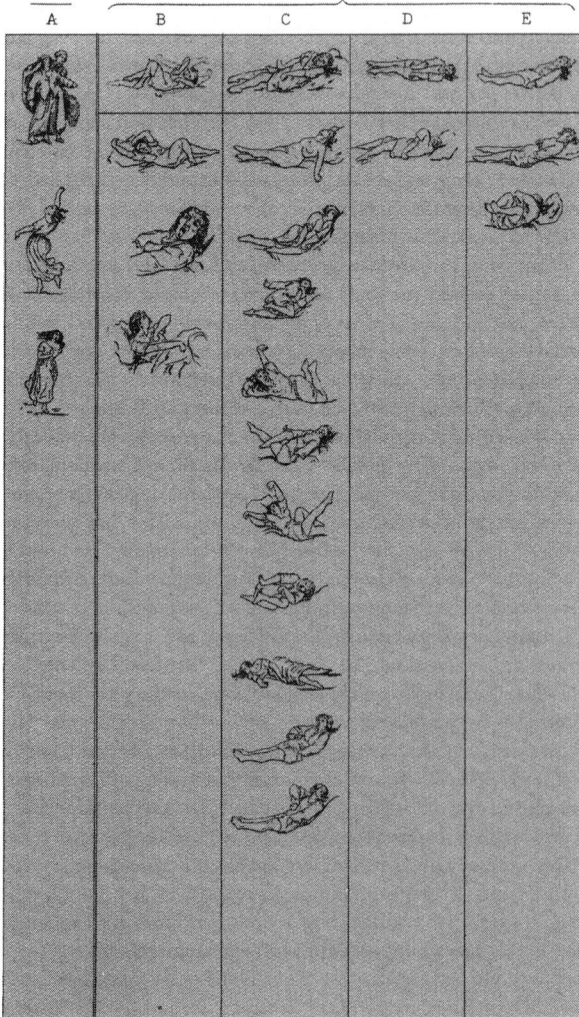

And I also wanted to talk to *you*.[1] Having watched your work again, and then watching *Syntagma*[2] this week, one of the questions for me was why film, and why this particular medium. It has always been one of the most challenging questions for me in terms of my engagement with the LUX Associate Artists Programme because I'm someone who only occasionally makes films. And so it was... I was remembering my interview and was thinking, why this context might be good—for *you*, given that you're someone who's a full-time regular filmmaker... That's *sort of* the background. [*Laughs.*] If you see what I mean.

LIS: Yes. I do see. [*Pause.*] It's a very difficult question to answer if you're asking me why do I make these things, I think it varies quite a bit. There's a lot of latitude if the idea of film is not defined before you start. And I think very often it is defined very narrowly. In 1982, 1983, Joanna Davis and I were making films for television.[3] They were actually meant to be shown among the ads but the content wasn't quite suitable, so they ended up in the legal department. The response to the work was that it wasn't television.[4] You think you're doing something, then you're told, actually, it isn't that, even though the videos were made specfically for television. Television it was. It wasn't. These contradictions are wonderful. You're

---

1   This conversation between Lis Rhodes and Emma Wolukau-Wanambwa took place at Kenwood House, a stately home in managed by English Heritage, on the afternoon of Friday 28 January 2011.

2   Valie Export, *Syntagma*, 1983, 16mm. Colour. 17 minutes

3   Lis Rhodes and Joanna Davis, *Hang on a Minute*, 1983–85, 13 one-minute films, 16mm. *Tyger Lily, Swing Song, Windscale, Ironing to Greenham, Washing Up, Goose and Common, Pornography, Words and Wealth, Pink Patterns, No.8 Bus, Much madness, White Words and Petal for a Paragraph with Rose English*, Music by Lindsay Cooper, Sung by Dagmar Krause.

4   "Channel 4 TV had just been established. Part of its remit was to support Film Workshops such as the Berwick St Film Collective, Cinema Action, Four Corners etc. Joanna and I made an application (1983) for a series called 'Hang on a Minute'. This was a few years before the commissioning of one – two or three minute films became a model for artists in the 1990s. The response from the legal department at Channel 4 was that 'they aren't television' – probably correct from their point of view. i.e there are rules – of appearance and meaning etc. However the actual reason gradually emerged, which was that the 'Hang on a Minute' in question was dealing with the mining group Rio Tinto Zinc's activities in Namibia. The editor at Ch.4 did not want to give an answering programme to the company. This is how I understood the situation at the time."
Lis Rhodes in email to Emma Wolukau-Wanambwa, 23 February 2011.

also describing something else, where there is a very prescribed *sort* of film, or an expectation of certain things. It is a problem, I think, with certain forms, with a certain language already laid down that may indeed not be very … sensitive to the questions you're asking.*

EMMA: Yes. Sure, I absolutely agree. Two things came up for me when you were saying that. One was the artist's film for Channel Four—*Three Minute Wonders* is the current incarnation. The Jarman Award winners get to make three-minute 'wonders'. One of the stipulations in the contract is that you can't have silence and you can't have black— (apparently)

LIS: I know. You can't. That's an old rule. They wouldn't show *Light Reading* [5] way back in 1986. No way.

EMMA: —because the first however many minutes is just voiceover.

LIS: That's right.

EMMA: Which is fascinating.

LIS: Isn't it? It's just…

[*LIS and EMMA laugh.*]

EMMA: I was always so fascinated by the test signal on television because it would come on to communicate that there was not communicating on. Even when they had nothing to show, they still had to say, 'Hello. We are not showing you anything.'

LIS: It is very, very, very interesting, isn't it?

EMMA: Yes. The thinking behind the knotty question I posed about film—which is really the question I'm asking myself—came out of two things. One has been following Ian White's inquiry into the place of film within the museum. (I think when he talks about the museum he is also talking actually about the canon—)

LIS: It sounds so.

---

5   Lis Rhodes, *Light Reading*, 1978, black and white 16mm. 20 minutes.

* "I think this refers to many parts of my work: the direct sense of language and the structures of grammar; the control of women in the 1980s in Britain through low or no waging; imprisonment for minor theft and the threat of insanity if women contravened the self-interest of the conservative establishment; and still (2009) which is silently and persistently still Rhodes, op.cit.

EMMA: Or an idea of art history, or something.

LIS: Art history rather than cinema history?

EMMA: Sure. I think that's one of the questions that informs me when I ask about the medium, the way I frame it for myself when I talk about why the moving image, or the conversation that I have with myself. It's about what that medium allows me to do in terms of duration, in terms of relationships (or non-relationships) between sound and image. It can be about sitting through something, about directing attention, ~~the~~ the kinds of decisions that can guide me towards ending up with moving image work. I was reminded of these things this week when I watched *Cold Draft*[6] and *Light Reading* again, and also looking at *Syntagma.* There is a connection — the use and re-use — a de-coupling. You can have the voice — one that makes use of the potentials of the medium ... sorry, this is all very waffly. [*Laughs.*] I'm ~~more~~ aware that when I ask these questions, there is a set of expectations that I bring to the idea of what a film is, or my received understanding of what a film is and how it works and how, what it represents and how it is represented and, in the context of this conversation particularly, how women figure in film.

REUSE – RECYCLE – RETOOL – RECOMBINE

also David Wojnarowicz, A fire in my belly and its often o, which he made with Ben Neil ... maktake break.

LIS: In some ways film has changed. We use the word 'film' — that's what I was just wondering about for a moment. In fact, what we are probably using now is something digital. One can now run umpteen versions of a finished work — which I could never afford to do when it was film. You did one and that was that! There are some things that are now extremely different, I think. Nothing *does* stay still and certainly film hasn't stayed still. And the shame is, of course, one loses the *readings* of these things too. There are losses — but interesting other things happen. But *they're very different things,* I think. When we use the word 'film,' it is a very difficult term. In a sense, it was interesting when you were referring to Ian and talking about the institution, and — perhaps — film within the gallery rather than film within the cinema. This is an old discussion. How much it all matters, I'm not very sure. I enjoyed it *most* very early on, when they were more interchangeable as an artist. One worked 'across', which I found much more interesting than ... <<INAUDIBLE>> ... sometimes I was working here, sometimes I was working there, and so on.

EMMA: That's why I am trying to *train myself to think*, or I'm trying to talk in terms — just for myself — of the moving image. To be *a bit more precise*.

---

6   Lis Rhodes, *Cold Draft*, 1988, 16mm.

* *(at least, in some part of the process)*

From: Emma Wolukau-Wanambwa
Subject: Re:
Date: 17 January 2011 12:32:15 GMT
To: Kate Davis

LIS: But it's a *terribly* imprecise term, isn't it? <u>No image ever actually moved</u> ←
<u>anywhere, as far as I know.</u> [*Laughs.*] It's one of the extraordinary things about
images—that they decay and they do change, but *they don't move.* [*Laughs.*]
Maybe I… <<INAUDIBLE>>

EMMA: Yes. ~~XXXX~~—you say they don't move, but I've been thinking—I've been
experimenting with very long exposures.

LIS: Ah!

EMMA: [*Laughs.*] Which sort of do something. ~~XXXXXXXXXXXX~~ $\overset{So}{U}$sing an eight-
minute or ten-minute exposure. Things like water become very interesting because
of the movement, and what happens over ten minutes from 'movement' *inside* an
image. [*Pause.*] I think this is going to be the year of long exposures. [*Laughs.*]

LIS: What does that mean in relationship to the sort… <<INAUDIBLE>> … it
brings up some questions about history, I think. Because that's an interesting way
of… thinking about history. Or inscribing it in some way?

EMMA: Yes. Inscribing some things but failing to capture others—I think is what
I'm interested in. Because$\overset{in\ such\ images}{\wedge}$some 'permanent structures' or 'permanent features' *can accrue*
this ~~XXX~~ immense solidity. Anything that happens too quickly just doesn't register on
the negative.$\underset{of\ the\ lens}{\wedge}$Landscape photographers do night shoots and they're able to wander *about in front*
~~XXXX~~ with torches and light bits of their composition, but you don't see them
because the aperture is open for so long. I think that's the reason I find them
interesting, these things that aren't being captured or don't register.[7]

LIS: 'Aren't being captured and don't register.'

EMMA: [*Pause.*] Yes. And I think—Again, this is a medium-specific conversation.
[*Laughs.*] I'm interested in capturing things that don't register within 'the frame'.[8]

→ *LIS:* Do you mean they're, sort of, <u>both present and absent *at the same time*</u>? ←

---

7   "I read this (maybe wrongly) as a metaphor for the 'permanent
structures or permanent features' overwriting the presence of anyone or
anything else." Rhodes, op cit.

8   "This seems to express a political position and a perception of
histories." ibid.

EMMA: I think … yes. [*Pause.*] If I stand in front of a waterfall, I will always have a different experience because of how many frames per second or whatever it is I see with my naked eye. It's going to look very different — even if I stand without blinking for ten minutes —

LIS: Indeed not. Because you're seeing differently. I was considering this wonderful phrase, 'the naked eye', and thinking I was yet to really meet one.

EMMA: So you've never seen an image that moves, and you've never seen a naked eye. [*Laughs.*]

LIS: I think that eyes are very highly educated, and trained. [Pause.]

EMMA: You know, the last time I tried to make a piece of work from this particular set of source materials, I became very interested in theories of learning to read — that is, in how we read, and in the relationship between the letter, its sound and its meaning, and in the ways in which those relationships are pretty arbitrary. There's nothing that says that that sort of shape [*draws the letter 'Z' in the air*] is a 'Z'. You could learn it as something else.

LIS: You certainly could.

EMMA: The fact that we have the Roman alphabet.. [*Laughs.*] These are all things you know, I'm sure.

LIS: No, but say them, because it's useful. The idea of what you've already learnt to see before you even start *looking*.

EMMA: I got these two books out of the library that were about the psychology of reading.[9] They were saying that when you read, it's actually about reducing probabilities. What you do when you read is try to reduce the number of possible options what the next word or the next letter is going to be. You work based on predictions. You're constantly predicting what's going to follow, you are always reading ahead of where you think you are on the page, and your ability to read something easily and fluently is apparently contingent on what it is that you already know about the subject

---

9   Keith Rayner & Alexander Pollatsek, *The Psychology of Reading*, New York: Prentice Hall, 1989. Frank Smith, *Understanding Reading: A Psycholinguistic Analysis of Reading and Learning to Read*, [4th edition] Hillsdale, New Jersey & Hove: Lawrence Erlbaum Associates, 1994.

matter. So, for example, ~~the~~ books ~~were stating~~ that children who are brought up in rural areas, surrounded by countryside and animals and the rest of it, will learn to read much more easily and more quickly if they read books about rural life. If they read books about urban life, they're not going to be able to ~~get~~ them because their predictions are not going to be so accurate. It's not necessarily about what you see in front of you, it's about all the things that precede your arrival at the page. The only time we do really read things is when we are reading things we know nothing about. If I had to read some very esoteric physics manual, I *have* to read every word and every letter—

LIS: How does this connect with translation, do you think?

EMMA: I don't know ... [*Pause.*] [*Laughs.*] I guess I'd say it's something that really interests me.

LIS: Me too. [*Laughs.*]

EMMA: Then you go first. Why does it interest you? [*Laughs.*]

LIS: For the very reasons you're saying. It's an entirely different sort of reading. It's not quite the same as when you were suggesting that you sat down to a pure mathematics book or something. I think it's different even to that. Which just goes to show that reading is very complicated and interesting. We can apply this to how we read images. Because I had a slightly different reading of her. [*Points at the painting.*] I thought she'd just finished speaking about whomever it was or whatever it was just there. [*Points.*]

[*EMMA laughs.*]

LIS: So it could have been she'd just finished doing this. [*Gestures.*]

EMMA: And then this moment. Yes.

LIS: It has a sort of—I wasn't *too* sure if by definition—I could read it the opposite way round to the reading you've suggested, or something. And I just wondered. Well, that's very interesting.

[*EMMA laughs.*]

LIS: We're both looking at the same thing. And we've both been educated in this way of looking this way but not that. And yet you can look very carefully at a single image—

[handwritten: In The Invention of Hysteria, Didi-Huberman says that Charcot deliberately discounted anything]

EMMA: —and have a totally different experience of it.

[handwritten: that his female patients in the asylum at Salpêtrière actually said. Just looking]

LIS: And I think it's *very* interesting.

[handwritten: at them naked, Charcot claimed, "told" him everything he needed to know.]

EMMA: The thing that got me when I first came here was her posture—the way she gestures away from herself. She's absolutely at the centre of the painting, but *[handwritten: our focus is directed outside the canvas (the frame).]* She's looking one way but pointing the other way. I found that extraordinary. I remember reading that when the painting was bought for this collection, they thought it was a Rembrandt. It's actually by Ferdinand Bol. At the time I came here, I really didn't know much about art or art history. I don't know if you can see, but in her hair, there's a bit of impasto I think is some sort of brooch or something. I remember looking at this enormous great lump of paint. I didn't know that it was deliberately applied by the artist, so I thought, 'it's the fakeness—it's the fakeness seeping out. It's the lie—it's the lie that it's not really a Rembrandt. Somehow, over the last 300 years the falsehood has just burst through the skin of the painting!' [*Laughs.*] Which is another *entirely* different reading that I had based on what I knew then. And then the last time I was here, the invigilator was telling me that they think it is one half of a marriage portrait. So this—

LIS: —this [*she imitates the gesture of the woman in the painting*] is not a gesture, it's an exhibition.

EMMA: Exactly. She's a sort of *[handwritten: "support"]* ~~brand~~. The actual subject of the painting is the ring. And the person she's looking at.

LIS: She doesn't look very enamoured of him. [*Pause.*] Do you write stories?

EMMA: Er…I do— *[handwritten: At least,]* I've started to *[crossed out]* *[handwritten: Because of this project I started researching in Uganda]* I came *[handwritten: last year]* back with this mess of stuff and I thought, 'I need to make something to help me to start to understand—unpick it, to unpick this experience and where the artwork lies and—what my position is in relation to it'. So I started—I *did* write. I have made one thing now from this material, a tiny installation.[10] It's about this size.

---

10   Emma Wolukau-Wanambwa, *Penderosa*, 2010, installation with 35mm slide, *[handwritten: slide viewer,]* ~~projector~~ inkjet print on paper, wood, matte black paint. *[handwritten: Overall dimensions 300mm × 300mm × 500mm.]*

[*Mimes.*] A little bit like the dioramas you made at school. It's got one slide in a slide viewer, which sort of looks like a little cinema.

LIS: A tiny cinema.

EMMA: Yes, but with one slide — one image that doesn't change. I've also written a text which is printed so it looks as if it's two pages of a book, but the rest of the book isn't there. Writing was initially just a way to start to think about the questions were in relation to this project: the relationship between fact and fiction, which we were talking about before, where the fiction of the project begins and ← ends, and what the fact of the project might be. And so... yes. I'm trying to do some writing.

LIS: I think that's quite important. [*Pause.*] It is interesting — this forcing of the end of a production before it's even started.

EMMA: Yes. It's difficult. [*Laughs.*]

LIS: This is the institution in another sense, isn't it? The institution that, in a sense, itself has to specialise.

I remember first learning about these debates in the context of live art practice — around the time when they were trying to

EMMA: Absolutely. ~~[struck through handwriting]~~

~ipline? formalise it as a <u>sector</u>, and what was at stake in trying to demarcate it as an area of practice. And that was about institutional recognition, and that was about —

└ and FUNDING

LIS: Protecting a history.

EMMA: Yes. Protecting a history, a history of practices that often fell between things. ~~Sub~~sequently, it's become an area of practice with its own 'borders', if you like.[11] But what's fascinating is how, say for example, performance has returned and become a more visible part of fine art practice again. But it doesn't necessarily have any relationship with those people who describe themselves as live artists, *who also make performance, sometimes even producing work with broadly similar form and content.*

LIS: Does it? There's a separation, you feel?

I understand so.

EMMA: ~~[struck through]~~ people I know who work in live art who talk about 'the

---

11   "Outside the borders – without institutional recognition – can you name yourself? Can you even claim to be or do?" Rhodes, op cit.

gallery circuit.' Not many people are able to do—are able to make that transition. It's interesting. *(Also some artists 'claimed' by both live art and fine art, eg. Marina Abramović.)*

LIS: It's interesting, isn't it?

EMMA: Yes. What 'naming' can do. [*Laughs.*]

LIS: 'What naming can do'. Indeed. I was wondering about live art and the 'capturing'—you were using the phrase or word 'capture'. And I was thinking, 'Imagine—of course, your *recent research trip* to Uganda', ~~Th~~There is the question of something live in a culture, the capturing of it and *maybe* the taking away—which, I'm sure is where you're at.

that I have started researching

EMMA: Absolutely. I wish I'd brought some images to show you now. There is a relationship between this body of framing and naming works that provides the context for this conversation and this project in Uganda. One of the things that struck me when looking at these *images of* the Alphabet, was to do with framing things, the naming, marking, defining of people—and indeed in the case of the [massacre]—marking people's fates on the basis of these processes of identification. When I was in Uganda I suddenly said to myself, 'is that not also what you are doing here?' I had all these 'hot topics' that I wanted to discuss—or I thought, 'oh this will be very sensitive. No one will want to talk about this'. Things that actually everyone was fine *about*, while other things, people ~~would~~ *were simply* bemus~~ing~~ed. A key moment for me came when there were two stories I had—'*stories*': that word '*stories*'—that I was wanting to put into this 'film': one which was to do with a house built by my great-grandfather in the 1930s—it's *enormous*. Well, I mean, we're sitting in Kenwood House. Kenwood House is enormous.

[*LIS and EMMA laugh.*]

EMMA: But, you know, compared to most of the others.

(I now think I might have been imagining those bullet holes. The only ones I definitely saw on a family home ~~was~~ were at Bweyogerere.)

LIS: Five or six bedrooms.

EMMA: Exactly. It's very large—in that part of Uganda, it's very unusual to see two-story *family homes* ~~houses~~. The last time I'd seen it, which was about 2001, it was in a really bad state. It still had bullet holes in the walls from the civil war, and the rest of it. I thought it was a very interesting house because it was built during a very particular moment of optimism about British Imperialism, in the 1930s. And everyone was 'fine'——well, certainly for *these people* things were kind of fine.

→ See Mary Bosworth, 'Confining Femininity: A History of Gender Imprisonment,' *Theoretical Criminology*, vol. 4, no. 3, pp. 265–84

a Massacre: *Gender, Power and Punishment in Revolutionary Paris*, Women, vol. 7, no. 10, October 2001, pp. 1101–21

(a reference to the slaughter of 35 women in the Parisian prison Conciergerie known as L'Hôpital de la Salpêtrière by armed men in September 1792. What 'marked' these particular female prisoners for death were the letters and symbols with which their bodies had been branded when they were sentenced.) ←

And what's happened since is written into the fabric of it. But I got there and the relative who now owns the house had done it up. All the bullet holes were covered over, and it looked shiny and new. I remember thinking, *'Oh no!'* —

[*LIS laughs.*]

EMMA: —and then *immediately* said, 'Emma—Stop! Now let's just think about that: why did you feel 'Oh no!'? What is at stake in you wishing this house to be in a particular state? Why is it a disappointment that its <u>history</u> has continued in 'evolution'? your absence? What does that tell you about the expectations you have brought with you here, and actually what might you be looking to find?[12] In a slightly weirdly self-interrogating way, that's the level at which I'm engaging with my materials now…[*Pause.*]..I think about the process of making. Or, what does 'making' mean? What's at stake in my own choices? What are the expectations that I bring to things when I am making them? It's that Nicholas Taleb phrase. Do you know Taleb?

LIS: No.

(I think)

EMMA: He's—what would you say?[13] [*Pause.*]… probabilities. He's one of these game theory people who became very rich and successful playing the stock market. He's written a book—a big seller called *Black Swan*.[14] And it is about events that aren't predictable and which can change the entire course of something.

(recognise the name)

LIS: I think I do. Did he … <<INAUDIBLE>> … there was a question of whether you could predict a gambling situation, and some people suggest you can.

EMMA: Maybe. But anyway—Taleb says that the predictions of financial analysts are really all nonsense. The <u>pertinent aspect of his critique</u>, however, is about the

(ie. for me — for this, not necessarily, perhaps for him)

---

12   "But what you did find was that traces of a condition had been replaced by a different condition – nothing except images stay still. That there has been an alteration of symptom still leaves the material causes unseen, unmarked, invisible." Rhodes, op cit.

13   Nassim Nicholas Taleb (b. 1960, Amioun, Lebanon) is a philosopher, essayist and practitioner of mathematical science. He is currently Distinguished Professor of Risk Engineering at the Polytechnic Institute of New York University.

14   Nassim Nicholas Taleb, *The Black Swan: The Impact of the Highly Improbable,* London: Allen Lane, 2007.

way in which we perceive — receive — information: what we see, what we look for, how sensitive we are. He talks about 'the confirmatory bias' — by which he means that rather than to be open to all the possible permutations and consequences of things, we have a tendency to look for and selectively focus on information that confirms what we already believe.

LIS: And you've gone to this building, to this house — even if you weren't thinking it, with certain expectations of…

EMMA: Yes. You bring … yes. You bring everything with you —

LIS: This is not 'the naked eye,' I think.

EMMA: Yes!

[*LIS and EMMA laugh.*]

EMMA: He's not someone I tend to have a lot of time for, but TS Eliot writes about it — how you bring everything you've ever read to every book you ever read.[15]

LIS: We do carry a lot of baggage. At my age, it gets quite heavy!

[*LIS and EMMA laugh.*]

LIS: I was very interested in the other image you sent me — the diagrams.[16] (looking at them,) I thought — this is what I actually wrote down: Where the woman is on her feet. The remaining 75, she is either —

[*EMMA and LIS together*]: — on her knees or on her back.

EMMA: Yes.

LIS: Now that is — if it isn't a male sexualised gaze — gazing and reporting on, I don't know what is.

---

15   TS Eliot, 'Tradition and the Individual Talent', 1919.

16   Letters A to L of Paul Richer's 'L'Alphabet d'Hysterie', in JM Charcot, *Etudes Cliniques Sur La Grande Hysterie ou Hystero-Epilepsie*, Paris 1885.

From: Kate Davis
Subject: Re:
Date: 23 January 2011 13:21:28 GMT
To: Emma Wolukau-Wanambwa

EMMA: That's given away by the image in the 'A1' position, which is the only one which shows a man, and he is physically restraining this woman. He's fully clothed, she's deshabillée.

LIS: Coming undone.

I understand that

EMMA: Yes. Coming undone. The really famous images from Salpêtrière are the photographs, which have been around, in discussion, in circulation, for a good *apparently* while now [17] — the discussion being about the extent to which they were posed or performed, and what was done to 'simulate' these postures that were subsequently recorded as scientific, objective fact. I find the drawings interesting because of the remove at which they (potentially) operate. The first time I ever saw them was in an exhibition at the Freud Museum, just down the road. I remember standing there for ages, thinking, they've tried to set down every single possible posture. Is there any movement I can make with my body that somehow will not find its place on this chart?'

LIS: These seem to me to be very very specific. Most women's lives are not very like that. At all. Surely he [18] would *like* them to be, but—

EMMA: [*Pause.*] Yes. There's all sorts of other bits of things that—

LIS: There's a few other things, like work. [*Laughs.*] It is very interesting how these things get written. I thought that was a piece of writing — in the sense we're talking about reading.

EMMA: [*Pause.*] This is a piece that is to do with writing and reading — what it is constructing and therefore inviting us 'to read', the way in which seeing these images in this context and the extent to which I might carry them into other… contexts, or other 'readings'.

LIS: But what is also interesting in that diagram is that you're moving it into a categorisation. So when we were talking a moment ago about reading and translation, reading and mathematics, you're actually moving it into something that can become abstracted to a degree that can be quite difficult to undo, which

17   See George Didi-Huberman, *Invention of Hysteria: Charcot and the Photographic Iconography of the Salpêtrière,* trans. Alisa Hartz, Cambridge Mass: MIT, 2003.

18   Paul Richer (1849–1933), the artist who created the Alphabet of Hysteria from the studies he made of Charcot's patients at L'Hôpital de la Salpêtrière

is a bit what I was talking about when I made *Light Reading*. The actual structure of grammar can do all sorts of things to a sentence, particularly if you use the word 'sentence', which might refer to one thing and might refer— *(← p.178)*

EMMA: —to something else. That's one of the things I was really excited about when I watched it again. This thing about what is read, or how these things can be reinterpreted ... The grammar or the legibility of an image even. There are sections where the image is split in half, or is brought back together again, when it seems to be one copy sitting on top of another, on top of another, on top of another one, and where the camera zooms in and out of particular sections of the image. Every time and in every context, the reading or the interpretation, or that which—even though it's the same 'thing'—the same source material, the permutations proliferate. That was one of the things I also found interesting looking at *Light Reading* in relation to the Valie Export film *Syntagma*, where she is also reuses particular images. And also filmes projections of them. It allows us to think about the different ways these things are read or are destabilised—or *can* be destabilised.[19] That's one of the really key words for me, looking at *Light Reading* and—actually, for me, I have to just come out and say it—the political potential of these things, of revealing their instability.

LIS: 'Revealing their instability' is a very interesting way of looking at it. Now, I think that is something I think is not understood perhaps—I feel—enough. [*Pause.*] Power is very dependent. [*Pause.*] Leave it at that.

EMMA [*Pause*]: I do agree with you.

LIS [*Pause*]: I brought you a poem. At the time, you were talking about voices, which I thought was precise and to the point. [*Pause.*] Do you know that one? [*Points.*]

EMMA: [*reads the poem silently.*] I don't know it. Is it Emily Dickinson?

LIS: Yes.

EMMA: I haven't come across this one.

LIS: Isn't it rather—?

19　"It is also the destabilising that happens in the act of reading as it is written." Rhodes, op cit.

From: Emma Wolukau-Wanambwa
Subject: Re:
Date: 27 January 2011 11:58:51 GMT
To: Kate Davis

Photographic segmentation

From: Kate Davis
Subject: Re:
   Date: 28 January 2011 20:52:25 GMT
      To: Emma Wolukau-Wanambwa

EMMA: It's fantastic. [*Reads aloud.*]
Much Madness is divinest Sense—
To a discerning Eye—
Much Sense—the starkest Madness—
'T is the Majority
In this, as All, prevail—
Assent—and you are sane—
Demur—you're straightways dangerous—
And handled with a Chain—[20]

LIS: Pretty accurate, I think.

EMMA: Very incisive.

LIS: Isn't it? And very interesting alongside those images, I thought.

EMMA: Just thinking about the reasons why those ‸women [poor, low status] ended up there in the first place.[21] [*Pause.*] And what <u>dissent</u>—well, just those kind of moments when things do and don't... Last year, I had the very great privilege of interviewing a sociologist called Stephanie Lawler, who is Reader in Sociology at the University of Newcastle. One of her main research topics is   the sociology of class. And she was talking about how middle-class identities work by the very principle that Emily Dickinson is talking about—that you stigmatise and expel that which is not—

LIS: The right shape and form.[22]

---

20   Emily Dickinson, 'Much Madness is Divinest Sense', c. 1862.

21   i.e. L'Hôpital de la Salpêtrière – in its incarnations as a prison and as an asylum. (It is now a public hospital.)

22   See Stephanie Lawler, 'Mobs and Monsters: Independent Man meets Paulsgrove Woman,' 2002, *Feminist Theory*, vol. 3, no. 1, pp. 103–113; 'Disgusted Subjects: The Making of Middle-Class Identities,' 2005, *The Sociological Review*, vol. 53, no. 3, pp. 429–446; 'The Middle Classes and their Aristocratic Others: Culture as Nature in Classification Struggles,' 2008, *Journal of Cultural Economy*, vol. 1, no. 3, pp. 245–261; and her book *Identity: Sociological Perspectives*, Cambridge: Polity Press, 2008. See also: Beverley Skeggs, 'The Making of Class and Gender through Visualizing Moral Subject Formation', *Sociology*, vol. 39, no. 5, 2005, pp. 965–82; Imogen Tyler, 'Chav Mum Chav Scum: Class Digust in Contemporary

EMMA: Yes. That's very much how class is about women's bodies. They are a key site of class formation, particularly for the middle classes. The idea of the 'ruly' and the 'unruly' body. Looking at the poem I was reminded of that. Dr Lawler was explaining how, within popular culture, the ways in which the borders are 'policed' — these areas of anxiety. Lampooning is a very key. people like Hyacinth Bucket, the television character,[23] for instance, and *Little Britain*[24], where images of abjection are summoned so we can express our anxieties and stigmatise and assert our '*distance from* ... the way in which something becomes marked. *Little Britain* is very interesting, actually, because a lot of it is about articulating the .veness of repulsi an unruly body — an overweight or ageing female body, a transvestite body, or even homosexual bodies. It's very much about stigma. It's very engaged with marking those things, where the humour comes from the marking of something as outside. Other. Well, humour for some people — I'm not including everybody in this.

LIS: 'Being observed' by the middle-classes has a correctness to it. I agree with that. power is a very curious one, I think, because there are different modes that mask each other. There's no doubt, to my mind, that wealth matters a very great deal. It can override a few other things. But I brought you another voice — following on from the reading of their bodies:

[LIS hands EMMA another text.[25] EMMA reads it silently. Pause.]

Britain', *Feminist Media Studies*, vol. 8, no. 1, 2008, pp. 17–34.

23   Hyacinth Bucket was the protagonist of the popular prime-time BBC sitcom *Keeping Up Appearances,* 1990–1995. Hyacinth is a grotesque social climber, whose attempts to attain middle-class respectability are thwarted by her vulgar working-class family, with whom she continues to maintain a relationship, whose existence she is unable to conceal, and whose behaviour she is unable to control. The sitcom, which written by Roy Clarke, ran for five series and 44 episodes. It only came to an end when it Patricia Routledge, who played Hyacinth, said she had had enough.

24   *Little Britain* is a character-based comedy sketch show that was first broadcast on BBC Radio 4 before being turned into a successful television series in 2003. It is written by and stars Matt Lucas and David Walliams. A large part of the show consists of parodies of people who already have very low social status.

25   'I believed in god; but when I saw so great an inequality between men, I acknowledged that it was not god who created man, but man who created god. And I discovered that those who wanted their property to be respected

*cf. Peter Stallybrass and Allon White, The Politics and Poetics of Transgression, Ithaca, New York: Cornell University Press, 1986

LIS: This is the slipperiness of sliding one thing to mask another thing.

EMMA: And it's to do with the collapse of social and economic circumstances onto identity, which is something that Stephanie Lawler is very —

LIS: Right. I'm totally with her, then. I think it runs through the question of madness and imprisonment.

EMMA: Absolutely. And it's about a collapse —

LIS: — and some very fast footwork.

EMMA: Yes. She and another bunch of sociologists of class who are working in this country — a very interesting intersection of class and education, by the way. One of the things they are tracking is the discourse of underclass in this country — the idea of an underclass and the *many and various institutional and discursive attempts to* *reclassify* *poor white* people essentially ~~as~~ *as* some kind of ethnic group.[26] So that there is a collapse. You can effect a collapse between — └ *"WHITE TRASH"*

LIS: This is boundaries again.

EMMA: Yes. And naming *So that social and economic disadvantage are reframed as having* nothing to do with what you are able to afford, or what opportunities are coming your way, *somehow* your own circumstances *can* become, *congruent* with your own failings. Stephanie's very interesting. she *traces this discourse at least* as far back as, say, Booth's 'Poverty Map of

---

have an interest in preaching the existence of paradise and hell, and in keeping the people in ignorance.' Emma Goldman, 'The Psychology of Political Violence', *Anarchism and Other Essays*, Third Revised Edition, New York: Mother Earth Publishing Association, 1917.

26   See: Tim Edensor and Steve Millington, 'Illuminations: Class Identities and the Contested Landscapes of Christmas', *Sociology*, vol. 43, no. 1, 2009, pp. 103–21; Chris Haylett, 'Illegitimate Subjects? Abject Whites, Neoliberal Modernisation and Middle-Class Multiculturalism', *Environment and Planning D: Society and Space*, vol. 19, 2001, pp. 351–70; Tracey Potts, 'Walking the Line: Kitsch, Class and the Morphing Subject of Value', *Nottingham University Modern Languages Publication Archive*, online; Diane Reay, et. al., 'A Darker Shade of Pale? Whiteness, the Middle Classes and Multi-Ethnic Inner City Schooling', *Sociology*, vol. 41, no. 6, 2007, pp. 1041–60; Beverley Skeggs, *Class, Self, Culture*, London & New York: Routledge, 2003.

London',[27] and the ways in which—if you look at the ~~designations~~ legend at the bottom of the map—they describe people as criminal. Right at the bottom. It's a map of poverty, but in the end they just say that these people are criminals. And it's the same: you are damned by—

LIS: —where you are. But that was said by the Metropolitan Police ~~during~~ about the student demonstrations. They said they were having to pull all their forces out of the work they should be doing on housing estates to deal with this other ... which is *exactly the same thing*.[28] That is the whole aim of policing is these—. So we mustn't lose history all together, I think.

EMMA: No. I'm not for—I'm very *pro* history in that sense.

LIS: [*Laughs.*] *Histories*, perhaps.

EMMA: Yes. I'm very pro ... if only because—

LIS: Because what?

EMMA: —if only because I'm so interested in what does and doesn't make it into the official version—I'm just going to quote it because it was the most fantastic

---

27   As part of his *Inquiry into the Life and Labour of the People in London,* 1886–1903, Charles Booth commissioned the 'Maps Descriptive of London Poverty'. Each street on the map is coloured to indicate the income and social class of its inhabitants according to a seven-tier classification system. The wealthiest, highest class inhabitants are represented by the yellow; the poorest, lowest class inhabitants are represented by black. The description of the 'black coloured' Londoners is as follows: 'Lowest class. Vicious. Semi-criminal'. See the *Charles Booth Online Archive*: http://booth.lse.ac.uk.

28   A reference to the widespread student-led demonstrations that took place across the UK in November 2010 in the run-up to the parliamentary vote to raise the cap on university tuition fees from £3,000 to £9,000. The demonstrators were protesting against the increase in tuition fees and the severe cuts to higher education spending that were being introduced. See Justin Davenport and Miranda Bryant, 'Met chief's fears for boroughs as beat officers are drafted in to student riots', *Evening Standard,* 14 December 2010.

phrase—'state sanctioned forms of history'—on Saturday there was a David Wojnarowicz event at Tate Modern[29]

LIS: Oh, absolutely. Dreadfully important.

EMMA: Which tells you very much about—the set of agendas and aspirations—and I think that for that reason alone we must be vigilant. And one must do one's reading. So one is aware of the histories and one is aware of that which is being chosen and that which is being omitted. And that was—

LIS: And yet we all have choice.

EMMA: [*Pause.*] Different degrees of choice. But … [*Pause.*] … yes.

[*Pause.*]

LIS: I meant that sarcastically.

EMMA: Oh good! I was just thinking, 'God—sure—'

[*They laugh.*]

LIS: I'm absolutely not sure at all.

EMMA: It's funny, I hadn't thought about it really until now, the dissertation I wrote at the end of my MA, when, obviously, for the record, I have to say you were my tutor.

LIS: So I was![30] [*Laughs.*]

---

29   There was an event at Tate Modern on Saturday 22 January 2011 at an event in support of the work of artist David Wojnarowicz, 1954–92, in the wake of a successful campaign by the Catholic League and US Congressman John Boehner to have Wojnarowicz's film 'A Fire in my Belly', 1986–87, removed from the exhibition *Hide/Seek: Difference and Desire in American Portraiture* at the National Portrait Gallery, Washington DC on the grounds it was blasphemous.

30   I studied for an MA in Fine Art (Sculpture) at the Slade School of Fine Art, University College London, 2006 to 2008. Lis Rhodes was my personal tutor.

EMMA: We've got to show our workings, you know. We can't pretend—

[*They laugh.*]

EMMA: —that I just happened to meet you in Kenwood House—

LIS: [*Laughing.*] I know.

EMMA: —that we've got no history.* *Our own history.* But, ~~such readings~~ about history. ~~and readings~~ and ~~memory~~ making, ~~and readings~~—The dissertation was to do with recent Second World War memorials.[31] There were two things that, in the context of this discussion, I recall ~~remember~~, one is that so many state memorials gesture away from themselves; they make no effort to preserve their own history,[32] in a really material, and practical sense. The papers aren't archived, their making is ~~making~~ not documented. All you have is the object, and the object is supposed to be everything. The fact that the object itself has a history is not something that features within their presentation in the public sphere. And two is the way in which memorials seek to preserve a particular historical moment.[33] So, say, all those Field Marshals outside the MOD, who did not die in their uniforms, but died many years later—we are going to remember them at this particular moment.[34] And the Women At War Memorial,[35] (which is where it all started for me, this whole subject) is just, basically, a lot of—

LIS: —clothes.

EMMA: —yes, clothes. On hooks. So the roles that women played in the war are

---

31   Emma Wolukau-Wanambwa, 'On Memorials, Remembrance and British National Identity', 2008.

32   See James E Young, *The Texture of Memory: Holocaust Memorials and their Meaning,* New Haven, Connecticut & London: Yale, 1993, pp. 11–12.

33   I would like to thank Andrew Walsh for pointing this out to me in 2005.

34   A reference to Ivor Robert-Jones's statues of Field Marshal Viscount Slim, 1891–1970, and Field Marshal Viscount Alanbrooke, 1883–1963, and Oscar Nemon's statue of Field Marshal Viscount Montgomery of Alamein, 1887–1976, which are installed in front of the Ministry of Defence Building, Whitehall, central London. All three men are depicted in military fatigues.

35   John W Mills's bronze Memorial to the Women of World War Two, 2005, is in the centre of Whitehall in central London.

* cf. Donna Haraway, 'Situated Knowledges: The science Question in Feminism, and The Privilege of Partial Perspective', *Feminist Studies*, vol. 14, no 3, pp 575–9.

on hooks. Effectively, the moment it's commemorating is not the active service of those women, but the moment *after* their return to the domestic sphere.

[Pause.]

KENWOOD HOUSE VISITOR OPERATIONS TEAM MEMBER:
Sorry, are you doing some sort of radio interview?

EMMA: Er…no. It's research—research for my…studies. That's all. It's not going to be broadcast anywhere.

KENWOOD HOUSE VISITOR OPERATIONS TEAM MEMBER: It's not going to be broadcast?

EMMA: No.

LIS: Not in the least.

KENWOOD HOUSE VISITOR OPERATIONS TEAM MEMBER: Fine. Okay.[36]

---

36   "A woman (a member of the same visitor operations team) sat in the gallery with us for the first hour without questioning us – i.e. she did not use the same authority has he did. She is absent from your transcript." Rhodes, op cit.

Portrait of Hannah Cullwick, framed, from the private collection of Arthur Munby

A.E.: Could you give an example of how you see her transforming social conditions with her cultural interventions?

R.L.: One of the photographs for instance shows a realistic scene and does not appear to have been created in a studio. It shows Hannah Cullwick on the steps of a doorway that obviously opens directly onto the street or to a pathway. The spectator finds him_herself as if he_she were a visitor to the house, before a large, black lacquered door, in front of which Cullwick is kneeling „on all fours." One feels reminded of the narration of Munby passing by the house and watching Cullwick cleaning the steps. Cullwick is turned toward the spectator with respect to the camera and looks directly at it. It seems as though she was photographed at her daily work, in the middle of cleaning the steps. I understand this photograph against the background of Kaja Silverman's use of the term „pose." Silverman introduces this term to mark the meaning of embodiment on the one hand and of visuality and photography on the other hand for the process of subjectivation. A „pose" is what a subject assumes when it is photographed. Taking over a pose, as Silverman argues, puts the subject who assumes it „in the picture." Embodiment is produced on the background of and „formatted through" a social archive of images. Letting oneself be photographed in the pose of a kind of work – as Cullwick did – which is barely recognized socially, can be then understood as a step toward subjugating oneself to an embodiment as a maid-of-all-work, and at the same time toward attaining subject status through this subjugation. The posing demands perception and recognition in this work. What interests me in Hannah Cullwick's cultural work is that she was able to smuggle some devices into the photograph that allude to the fact that she is not only undertaking the pose of a house maid but at the same time a pose that can be read in the context of her SM relationship: She is not only throwing a gaze back to the spectator very self-confidently but she also presents her „slave band" almost in the center of the image, a black leather band which was a sign of her position as a „slave" in her relationship with Munby. I would claim that Hannah Cullwick's sexual posing allows for a kind of queering agency, precisely because it mimetically copied the image of the domestic servant. The photograph becomes a kind of picture puzzle, which allows for the subject to be recognized as much as it appears to indicate a self-authorization in the fields of sexuality and work. In this way, Hannah Cullwick created representations that double the image of the domestic servant, but that also „disrupt" or „queer" it.

Extracts from Antke Engel, 'Interview with Pauline Boudry and Renate Lorenz', *Normal Work*, Berlin: B-Books, 2008

LIST OF CONTRIBUTORS
AND
ARTIST BIOGRAPHIES

Mina Bancheva

is a psychotherapist who works for the Priory Hospital, Keats Clinic, London and she runs a private practice in Bath. Born in Sofia, Bancheva moved to the UK in 1968. She maintains an interest in art and writing.

Pauline Boudry / Renate Lorenz

work with film, video, photography, installation, and text which incorporate and reflect upon the historical archives of photography and film. Their practice focuses on the history of sex, gender discourses and practices, and the meaning of 'visibility' since early modernity.

Christoph Cox

is Professor of Philosophy at Hampshire College and a faculty member at the Center for Curatorial Studies, Bard College. The author of *Nietzsche: Naturalism and Interpretation* (California, 1999) and co-editor of *Audio Culture: Readings in Modern Music* (Continuum, 2004), Cox writes regularly on contemporary art and music for *Artforum, The Wire* and other magazines.

Kate Davis

is an artist based in Glasgow. Davis works across a range of media, including drawing, installation, bookworks and film. Informed by successive waves of feminist art and theory, her practice centres on the fragile re-calibration of representation through twentieth-century art history and literature. Davis is a part-time lecturer at Glasgow School of Art. Solo shows include Museo de la Ciudad and La Galeria de Comercio, Mexico; Kunsthalle Basel; Art Now, Tate Britain, London, 2007. Residencies include Cove Park, in Argyll and Bute, Scotland; Banff Arts Center, Canada and Camden Arts Centre, London.

Éric La Casa

is a sound artist. For over fifteen years his musical practice has been a series of experimentations/improvisations with this sonic locale. As it passes through his microphones, the site of the survey — everyday life — is transformed into a site of play. The dimensions of the real world generate sonic representations whose proportions found another perspective on the world. ascendre.free.fr

Lars Bang Larsen

is an art historian at the University of Copenhagen. He has co-curated exhibitions such as Populism (2005), *La insurección invisible de un millón de mentes* (2005) and *A History of Irritated Material* (2010). His books include *The Model. A Model for a Qualitative Society* (1968) (2010)

Isla Leaver-Yap

is a writer and curator based in New York. At ICA, London, she co-organised *Nought to Sixty,* the UK's largest survey of emerging contemporary art, and organised projects with artists including Rosalind Nashashibi, Fia Backström and Mark Leckey. She has curated projects for Tramway, Glasgow; Anthology Film Archives, Chrysler Series, Calder Foundation and Sculpture Center, New York. She is the editor of *MAP* magazine and writes for *Afterall, Mousse* and other titles. She is a member of CAGE, New York.

Uriel Orlow

is a senior research fellow at University of Westminster, London. Orlow is currently working on exhibition projects for the Swiss Pavilion, 54th Venice Biennale; 8th Mercosul Biennial, Brazil; ACAF Alexandria and FRAC Aquitaine Bordeaux. Previous exhibitions and screenings include: Tate Modern and Gasworks, London; 3rd Guangzhou Triennial, Guangdong Museum of Art; South African National Gallery Cape Town; Jewish Museum, New York; Les Complices Zurich; International Short Film Festival Oberhausen; Argos, Brussels.

Dominic Paterson

teaches modern and contemporary art and theory at the University of Glasgow. Dr Paterson has written essays on artists such as Christine Borland, Lucy Gunning, Claire Barclay, Martin Soto Climent, Kate Davis and Faith Wilding. He is a regular contributor to *MAP* magazine, and in 2010 organised a series of film screenings and talks for Glasgow International.

Lee Patterson

attempts to understand his surroundings by using both the aided
and the naked ear. Recent commissions include *Bouillon de Sons
Frioulais, Marseille; Catchments (for The Glen and The Till)*,
Newcastle; and *A Grammar for Listening* with Luke Fowler. He is
currently artist-in-residence at Stour Valley Arts, Kent. Solo
releases include *Egg Fry #2* and *Seven Vignettes. Wunderkammmern*
with David Toop and Rhodri Davies was released in December 2010.
He lives in Prestwich.

Lis Rhodes

is an artist and filmmaker. She studied at the North East London
Polytechnic and the Royal College of Art. From 1975–76 Rhodes was
the cinema curator of the London Filmmakers' Co-operative. As an
active campaigner for women's rights, Rhodes was a founder member
of Circles, a women's artist film and video distributor began in
1979. She lives and works in London.

Deborah Stratman

is a Chicago-based filmmaker and artist interested in landscapes
and systems. Recent and upcoming projects address manifest
destiny, freedom, sonic warfare, faith, the paranormal, African
media propagation and the oracular history of comets. Stratman has
exhibited and been awarded internationally at venues including
MoMA, Pompidou, Hammer Museum, Whitney Biennial, Sundance,
Viennale, Oberhausen, L'Alternativa and Rotterdam.

Maija Timonen

is a filmmaker and writer based in London. The formal scope of her
films ranges from montages of casually recorded video footage to
carefully orchestrated cinematic scenes. She has a PhD from the
Slade School of Art, London, where her research dealt with
concepts of authorship in relation to filmmaking and contemporary
institutional art environments. Often using literary sources as
starting points, her practice approaches text and images in a
dissective manner. A breakdown of form and its partial reconstruc-
tion is used to inquire into the legacies of Modernism, with the
political potential of their retrieval as a guiding concern.

Toshiya Tsunonda

is a sound artist based in Yokohama. He runs Skiti, a label for experimental composition, and private label called edition.t. Recent exhibitions and performances include: *Displaced Sounds,* STUK, Belgium,
2010; *Half Life,* Kilmartin Glen, Argyll, 2007; and a collaboration
with Luke Fowler at Yokohama Triennale, 2008. His CD output
includes: *Low Frequency observed at Maguchi Bay,* hibari; *Scenery
of Dacalcomania,* Naturestrip; and *Ridge of Undulation,* Hapna.

Marina Vishmidt

is a writer engaged in questions relating to art, labour and the
value-form. She is studying a PhD on 'Speculation as a Mode of
Production in Art and Capital' at Queen Mary University, London.
Recent research includes a residency with FRAC, Lorraine, and a
Jan van Eyck Academy fellowship. She is co-editor of *Uncorporate
Identity* (Baden: Lars Müller, 2010), and Media Mutandis: Art,
Technologies and Politics (London: Node, 2006). She contributes to
catalogues, edited collections and journals such as Mute,
Afterall, and *Texte zur Kunst.* She also takes part in Unemployed
Cinema, Cinenova and Signal:Noise.

Judith Williamson

is a writer and broadcaster on contemporary culture and politics.
She is the author of *Decoding Advertisements: Ideology and Meaning
in Advertising, Consuming Passions: The Dynamics of Popular
Culture* and *Deadline at Dawn: Film Criticism 1980–1990* (London:
Marion Boyars, 1978, 1986 and 1993 respectively).

Luke Fowler
Born Glasgow, 1978
Based in Glasgow

Selected solo exhibitions
2012   The Hepworth, Wakefield
2010   *Ways of Hearing,* IMO,
       Copenhagen
2009   *A Grammar for Listening,*
       Serpentine, London
—   *RWarriors: Four Films,*
       X Initiative, New York
2008   Kunsthaus, Zürich
2006   *Pilgrimage From Scattered
       Points,* White Columns,
       New York
—   *The Nine Monads Of David
       Bell,* Villa Concordia, Bamberg
2000   *How Did You Get This Number?,*
       Generator, Dundee
—   *The Social Engineer,*
       Transmission, Glasgow

Selected group exhibitions
/ screenings
2010   *In The Days Of The Comet,*
       British Art Show 7,
       Nottingham Contemporary
       Hayward, London,
       Tramway, Glasgow
—   *ACT VI: Remember Humanity,*
       Witte de With, Rotterdam
2009   *ourtv,* Lothringer13,
       Städtische Kunsthalle, Munich
—   *Radical Nature,* Barbican,
       London
—   *Running Time: Artists Films
       in Scotland 1960 to Now,*
       Dean, Edinburgh

—   *The Associates,* DCA, Dundee
—   *Younger than Jesus,*
       New Museum, New York
2008   Yokohama Triennale
       (with Tsunoda Toshiya)
2008   International Film Festival,
       Rotterdam (screening)
—   *Expanded Cinema for Rothko,*
       The Room, Tate Modern,
       London
—   *Kill Your Timid Notion,*
       DCA, Dundee
2007   East International, Norwich
—   *Lost and Found,* Shedhalle,
       Zurich
—   *Never Still,* MAP magazine
       at CCA, Glasgow (screening)
—   *Organizing Chaos,* PS1,
       New York
—   *Twilight Adventures in Music,*
       Whitechapel, London
       (screening)
—   *You Have Not Been Honest,*
       Museo d'Arte Contemporanea
       Donnaregina, Naples
2006   Tate Triennial, Tate Britain,
       London
2005   *Becks Futures,* ICA, London
2004   *Past Imperfect,* Casco, Utrecht
2003   *Zenomap,* Scottish Pavillion,
       Venice Biennale
2002   Manifesta 4, Frankfurt

Awards / residencies
2008   Derek Jarman Award
—   Grierson Archive,
       Stirling (residency)
2006   Internationales Künstlerhaus
       Villa Concordia, Bamberg,
       Germany (residency)

2005 Kenchington / Gilbert Scott,
      Balfron, Scotland (residency)
2004 Donald Dewar Prize
2002 NIFCA, Helsinki (residency)

Selected bibliography
—   *Luke Fowler,* Zürich: JRP
      Ringier, 2009
—   George Clark, 'The way out is
      via the door', *Mousse,* no. 18,
      April 2009
—   Sarah Lowndes, *Spike,* no. 20,
      May 2009
—   Martin Herbert, 'The Way In',
      MAP, no. 18, Summer 2009
—   Luke Fowler, 'Life in Film',
      Frieze, no. 106, May 2007
—   Chris Rose, *The Wire,* no. 254,
      April 2005

Laura Gannon
Born Galway, 1972
Based in London

Selected solo exhibitions
2010 *World/Interior,* Arts Centre,
      Ballina
2009 *Jewelled Eagle,* Sketch,
      London
2007 *A house in Cap-Martin,*
      Whitechapel Project Space,
      London
2003 *Wordsong,* Hugh Lane, Dublin

Selected group exhibitions
/ screenings
2011 *Enter slowly,* The Lab,
      San Francisco
2010 *Deschooling society,* Hayward,
      London (screening)
2010 *Indian Summer,* Espace
      Croise, France
2010 *Claremorris Open,* Claremorris
2010 *West Cork Arts Centre,* Cork
2008 *Showtime,* Gasworks, London
2007 *Bloomberg Art Futures,*
      London
2004 *No.w.here,* London
2004 *Timepop,* Prince Charles
      Cinema, London
2003 *Onufri Prize,*
      National Gallery, Tirana
2001 *Enter,* Gerokstrasse 37,
      Stuttgart
2001 East International, Norwich

Selected bibliography
—   Dewitt Cheng: 'Enter Slowly',
      Visual Art Source, Feb 2011

— Matthew Marchand, 'Enter slowly', *Art Practical, 2.11 / Geography Lessons,* Feb 2011

— Noel Kelly and Seán Kissane, *Creative Ireland: The Visual Arts in Ireland 2000 to 2010,* Dublin: Visual Artists Ireland, 2011

— Brian Dillon, 'Decline and Fall', *Frieze,* no. 130, April 2010

— Vincent Honoré, 'A house by the sea', *Circa,* no. 122, Winter 2007

— Barbara Dawson, *Wordsong,* Dublin: City Gallery, Hugh Lane, 2003

— Declan Long and Aidan Dunne, *Anois,* Dublin: Temple Bar, 2001

Duncan Marquiss
Born Dumfries, 1979
Based in London

Selected solo exhibitions
2011 Sorcha Dallas, Glasgow
2009 *There Is No You,* Galerie Peter Kilchmann, Zurich
2007 *The Clay Wall,* Changing Room, Stirling
2004 *Night Music,* Dicksmith, London

Selected group exhibitions / screenings
2011 *Secret Societies,* Schirn Kunsthalle, Frankfurt & CAPC musée d'Art contemporain de Bordeaux
2011 *Difficult Gifts,* MAP magazine at E-flux, New York (screening)
2010 *Serpentine Cinema: CINACT,* The Gate Cinema, London (screening)
2009 *Running Time: Artist's Films in Scotland 1960 To Now,* Dean, Edinburgh
— *The Associates,* DCA, Dundee
2007 *Strange Weather,* Neuer Berliner Kunstverein, Berlin (screening)
2006 *What Am I Doing Here?,* Galleria Civica di Arte Contemporanea Montevergini, Sicily
2005 *Antitheticals,* International Biennale of Contemporary Art, National Gallery, Prague
2003 *Zenomap,* Scottish Pavilion, Venice Biennale (screenings)

Selected bibliography
— Will Bradley, 'The Clay Wall',
  exhibition text, 2007
— Duncan Marquiss,
  'MicroTate', *Tate etc.,* no. 11,
  Autumn 2007
— Eliza Williams, 'The Clay
  Wall', *Flash Art,* no. 252,
  Jan–Feb 2007
— Yannis Tsitsovits, 'Duncan
  Marquiss', *Stimulus Respond,*
  vol. 1, 2007
— Sarah Lowndes, 'Duncan
  Marquiss', London: Frieze
  Art Fair Year Book 2006

Laure Prouvost
Born Lille, 1978
Based in London

Selected solo exhibitions
2011 *before, before. before it was,*
     the title sequence, spinning
     before next, a squid,
     MOT International, London
—   *Time Machine,* Bookworks,
     Spike Island, Bristol and IPS,
     Birmingham
2010 *All These Things Think Link,*
     Flat Time House, London
—   *Art Now Lightbox,*
     Tate Britain, London
2009 *Storeybored,* After the Butcher,
     Berlin
—   *Burrow Me,* Lighthouse,
     Brighton.

Selected group exhibitions
/ screenings
2011 *Time Again,* Sculpture Center,
     New York,
—   *Department Of Wrong Answers,*
     Wysing Arts, Cambridge
—   *Light Writing,* Banner
     Repeater, London
—   *Museum of Speech,* Extra
     City-Kunsthal Antwerpen,
     Belgium
—   *Difficult Gifts,* MAP magazine
     at E-flux, New York (screening)
2010 *Strong Sory,* Look, Budapest
—   *More Pricks Than Kicks,*
     David Roberts Art
     Foundation, London

— *Now Then___*, E:vent Gallery,
London
— *New Contemporaries*, ICA,
London, and A Foundation,
Liverpool
— *Kryptonim Matrioszka,*
Bunkier Sztuki, Krakow
— International Kurzfilmtage,
Oberhausen (screening)
— International Film Festival,
Rotterdam (screening)
2009 *The Know Unknows,*
Whitechapel, London
— *The Filmic Conventions,*
FormContent at Zoo Art
Fair 2009, London
— East International, Norwich
— London Film Festival,
BFI, London (screening)

— Laure Prouvost,
Novel, no. 3, 2010
— Sally O'Reilly, *Art Monthly,*
no. 341, Nov 2010
— Colin Perry, 'Laure Prouvost',
Frieze, no. 132, June–Aug 2010
— Adrian Searle,
'East International plays fast
and loose with the truth',
The Guardian, 20 July 2009

Awards / residencies
2011 FLAMIN, London
— Wysing Arts Center residency,
Cambridge
— CCA Residency, Glasgow
2010 International Kurzfilmtage,
Oberhausen Short Film
Principal Prize
2009 East award,
East International, Norwich

Selected bibliography
— Francesco Pedraglio, 'The Floor
is Slippery, Is There Anything
We Can Hold On To?',
Mousse, no. 26, Nov 2010

Grace Schwindt
Born Frankfurt, 1979
Based in London

Selected solo exhibitions
2011 *Signal,* South London
     Gallery, London
     (performance)
2010 *Counterpoint 1, part 1:*
     The individual account, ICA,
     London (performance)
—   International
     Kurzfilmtage, Oberhausen
—   White Columns, New York

**Selected group exhibitions
/ screenings**
2010 International
     Kurzfilmtage, Oberhausen
     (screening)
2009 *It's hard to find the beginning,*
     and impossible to fathom
     the end, Trafo, Budapest
—   East International, Norwich
—   *Freshfacedandwildeyed,*
     Photographers' Gallery,
     London
—   *The Neutrality of this Section*
     is Disputed, Athens Biennale
—   *Salon 09,* S1 Artspace,
     Sheffield

Awards
2010 FLAMIN, London
—   Travel scholarship, Boise
—   Travel grant, British
     Council

Selected bibliography
—   Isla Leaver-Yap, *Mousse,*
     no. 29, June 2011

Samuel Stevens
Born Nottingham, 1978
Based in London

**Selected group exhibitions
/ screenings**
2011 *ONVI desrealitat,* Centre
     de Cultura Contemporània
     de Barcelona, Barcelona
2010 *Frieze Film,* Frieze Art Fair,
     London (screening)
—   Ann Arbor Film Festival,
     Michigan (Best False Fiction
     Jury Award)
—   *Leaving Room,* Centro
     culturale francese di Palermo
     e della Sicilia, Sicily
     (screening)
—   *CINACT: Serpentine*
     Cinema, The Gate Cinema,
     London (screening)
2009 *Darklight Festival,* Dublin
     (screening)
—   *Transmission Interrupted,*
     Modern Art Oxford, Oxford
     (screening)
2008 Guangzhou Triennial,
     Guangdong Museum of Art,
     Guangzhou (screening)
—   *E-flux Video Rental,*
     Building, Berlin
—   *Goodgangsters,* Taipei
     Museum of Fine Art, Taipei
2007 International Istanbul
     Biennial, Istanbul (screening)
     Vocal Verbal, Galerija SC,
     Zagreb (screening)
2006 *Performing the Truth,* Studio 27,
     San Francisco (screening)

— *Oral Actions,* Overtones,
Los Angeles (screening)
— *New Semantics,* Whitechapel,
London (screening)
— *Karownale,* Cinema ACUD,
Berlin

Awards
2008 FLAMIN, London

Selected bibliography
— Stephen Connolly, 'When
I Sit Down to Write, On
Two Films by Samuel
Stevens', *When I Sit Down,*
Ed. Samuel Stevens, London:
Pamphleteer Films, 2010
— Eds. Birgit Ludwig and
Laure Prouvost, *Fresh
Moves: New Moving Images
from the UK,* London: Tank
tv / Thames & Hudson, 2007
— Stuart Comer, 'Looking
Back: Emerging Artists',
Frieze, no. 107, January 2007

Stina Wirfelt
Born Gothenberg, 1980
Based in Glasgow

Solo exhibitions
2010 +44141, Glasgow

Selected group exhibitions
/ screenings
2011 International Film Festival,
Rotterdam (screening)
— Filmfest DC, Washington DC
(screening)
— IndieLisboa, Lisbon (screening)
2010 *Hello World,* Embassy,
Edinburgh
— *Walls Of Light,* CCA,
Glasgow (screening)
— *The Stones of Menace,* St.
Paul's Bow Common, London
— *The Bag of Tricks Show,*
Intermedia, Glasgow
— *X-Ray at Supermarket,*
Stockholm
2009 *ourtv,* Lothringer Straße 13,
Munich
— *Invisible Square,*
Transmission, Glasgow
— *Filmform,* Gävle and
Stockholm (screening)
— *Flytande Ögonblick,* Ystads
Konstmuseum
2008 *Samtida Videokonst,*
Jönköping
— *Tipsa En Vän,* Bonniers
Konsthall, Stockholm
— *Unclassifiable,* Overgaden,
Copenhagen (screening)
— Galleri 54, Hagateatern,
Gothenberg (screening)

— *The State,* Glasgow
International
— *Cast some light,* Glasgow
International (screening)
— *At Our Hands,*
Project Room, Glasgow
2007 *Sfumatura della Palindrome,*
A Vermin, Glasgow
— *Crosskick,* Kunstverein,
Hannover
— *Curious Green,* Circus
Gallery, Los Angeles
— *Loop,* Hotel Catalonia
Ramblas, Barcelona
— *Unclassifiable,* LMCC,
New York

Selected bibliography
— Alhena Katsof, 'Stina Wirfelt',
MAP, no. 18, Summer 2009

Emma Wolukau-Wanambwa
Born Glasgow, 1976
Based in London and Bad Ems

Solo exhibitions
2008 *A Brush for Robben Island,*
Butchers Projects at Rokeby,
London

Selected group exhibitions
/ screenings
2011 *Chewing the Scenery,*
Swiss Pavilion, Venice
Biennale (screening)
— *Iceploitation,* Kunstforening,
Tromsø (screening)
— *Nothing Personal,* Marcelle
Alix, Paris
2010 *Públicos y Contrapúblicos,*
Centro Andaluz de Arte
Contemporaneo, Seville
— *Whose Map Is It?,* Iniva,
London
2009 *Indirect Speech,* Night Sessions,
Intermediae, Madrid
(screening)
— *Complex Financial Instruments,*
S1 Artspace, Sheffield
(screening)
— *Where is Now?,*
Württembergischer
Kunstverein, Stuttgart
(screening)
2007 International Kurzfilmtage,
Oberhausen (screening)
2006 *Bang Hwang Ha Num Byul:
British-Korean Landscape,*
Gana, Seoul
— *For One Night Only,* Camden
Arts Centre, London

Selected bibliography
—   Deborah Schultz, 'Whose
     Map Is It? New Mapping by
     Artists: Iniva, London',
     Art Monthly, no. 338,
     July–August 2010
—   Patricia Bickers, 'Selected
     Pieces: A Brush for Robben
     Island by Emma Wolukau
     Wanambwa', *Catalogue*,
     no. 3, March 2010
—   Sacha Craddock, 'Emma
     Wolukau-Wanambwa',
     Wandering Star, Seoul: Gana
     Art Gallery, 2006

COLOPHON

8 METAPHORS (because the moving image is not a book)
Published 2011

A book by Luke Fowler, Laura Gannon, Duncan Marquiss, Laure Prouvost,
Grace Schwindt, Samuel Stevens, Stina Wirfelt, Emma Wolukau-Wanambwa

Edited by Isla Leaver-Yap
Designed by HIT
Printing and binding by LULU.com

Éric La Casa translated By Owen Martell;
Grace Schwindt and Marina Vishmidt transcribed by Amy Liptrot;
Toshiya Tsunoda translated by Yuko Zama

All contributions appear courtesy the artists and as follows:
Kate Davis, Sorcha Dallas, Kamm; Luke Fowler, Modern Institute; Éric
La Casa, Isabelle Gounod; Duncan Marquiss, Sorcha Dallas, Peter
Kilchmann; Laure Prouvost, MOT. Stina Wirfelt's participation in AAP
is supported by IASPIS, Stockholm

ISBN: 978-0-9567941-3-0

LUX
Shacklewell Studios
18 Shacklewell Lane
London, E8 2EZ
Tel: +44 (0)20 7503 3980

The artists and editor would like to thank the contributors,
the artists' representatives, and the following individuals for their
invaluable advice and support: Lina Grumm, Stewart Home, Annette Lux,
Gregor Muir, Ian White